LANDMARK CASES

CASES

12 Historic Supreme Court Decisions

LANDMARK CASES

12 Historic Supreme Court Decisions

— A Companion to the C-SPAN Series —

TONY MAURO

Introduction by Jeffrey Rosen, National Constitution Center

Landmark Cases is published by National Cable Satellite Corporation in cooperation with CQ Press, an imprint of SAGE Publications, Inc. All cases contained herein originally published in *Illustrated Great Decisions of the Supreme Court, Second Edition*, by Tony Mauro. © 2006 CQ Press, an imprint of SAGE Publications, Inc. Reprinted by permission. See: www.sagepub.com.

sagepub.com

Cover design and layout by Ellen Vest, C-SPAN

TONY MAURO has covered the Supreme Court for 35 years, first for Gannett News Service and *USA TODAY* and then, since 2000, for *Legal Times, The National Law Journal*, and now *Supreme Court Brief*, a subscription newsletter about the court.

Mauro received a bachelor's degree in political science from Rutgers University, and a master's degree from the Columbia University Graduate School of Journalism. *Washingtonian* magazine has twice included Mauro on its list of the top 50 journalists in Washington. He is a longtime member of the steering committee of the Reporters Committee for Freedom of the Press, and in 2011 was inducted into the Freedom of Information Act Hall of Fame in recognition of his advocacy for openness in courts and other government institutions.

The case descriptions in this book are drawn and updated from the second edition of Mauro's book *Illustrated Great Decisions of the Supreme Court*, published in 2006 by CQ Press, an imprint of SAGE Publications, which gave permission for its use.

⚖️

JEFFREY ROSEN is president and chief executive officer of the National Constitution Center, the only institution in America chartered by Congress "to disseminate information about the United States Constitution on a non-partisan basis." Rosen is also a law professor at the George Washington University Law School. A contributing editor of the *Atlantic Monthly*, he is a longtime legal affairs commentator whose essays and commentaries have appeared in *The New York Times Magazine, The New Republic*, on National Public Radio, and in *The New Yorker*. He is the author of several books about the Court and the Constitution, including the forthcoming *Louis D. Brandeis: American Prophet*.

TABLE OF CONTENTS

FOREWORD

The first Monday in October is the traditional opening of the Supreme Court's new term. In 2015, it falls on October 5, and on that same day C-SPAN, in cooperation with the National Constitution Center, embarks on a new twelve-part historical television series that will tell the stories behind some of the Court's most significant cases.

Landmark Cases: Historic Supreme Court Decisions examines a dozen cases that shaped the Court's role in American society, or helped change our society itself. In this book, the words of veteran Supreme Court journalist Tony Mauro help set the stage for the series with brief introductions to the backgrounds, highlights, and impact of these cases. We begin the series with *Marbury v. Madison*, which Justice Ruth Bader Ginsburg calls the Court's most famous decision, for its role in establishing the principle of judicial review. We end it with the 1973 decision in *Roe v. Wade*, a case whose ramifications continue to play out in the public sphere. There is also *Schenck v. United States* which gave rise to the famous judicial assertion that even under our First Amendment protections, one can't "falsely shout fire in a theater," establishing the principle that free speech isn't absolute; and there is *Youngstown Sheet & Tube Co. v. Sawyer*, which limited the power of presidents to seize private property, even in time of war.

Landmark Cases gives special emphasis to the individuals whose judicial appeals gave rise to these momentous decisions. Their stories clearly emphasize that from its inception the Court sought to offer redress not only to the well-connected and powerful, but to slaves seeking freedom (*Scott v. Sandford*), to black children seeking equality of education (*Brown v. Board of Education of Topeka*), and to convicted criminals who believed their prosecutions were unfair (*Mapp v. Ohio; Miranda v. Arizona*). The accessibility of the high court to all petitioners stands as a powerful statement about the American judicial process.

While it may be available to petitioners from all walks of society, the Court is hardly infallible in its decisions. *Landmark Cases* illustrates this through the story of Missouri slave Dred Scott. In 1857, the Court's decision in his case denied citizenship to African Americans and contributed to the start of the Civil War. This terrible ruling held fast until the Thirteenth and Fourteenth Constitutional Amendments settled the issue, abolishing slavery and establishing full citizenship for former slaves. There is also the story of Fred Korematsu, a Japanese American citizen interned in a government camp during World War II, a policy sanctioned by a 1944 Court ruling. Decades later, to underscore the wrongness of the program and of the Court's approval of it, the federal government formally apologized for its internment policy and belatedly created a victims' compensation fund. And, in a measure of personal justice for Fred Korematsu, his conviction was overturned in 1983 and in 1998 he was awarded the Presidential Medal of Freedom.

These twelve stories will be told by C-SPAN in the network's signature programming style — a mix of you-are-there visits to historic sites associated with each case, interviews with historians and Court experts, and audience interaction through social media and viewer phone calls. All of our video and contextual information, along with lesson plans for classroom use, will be permanently available on the series' website, www.c-span.org/landmarkcases.

Mark Farkas, producer of C-SPAN's Peabody Award-winning *American Presidents*, is the executive producer of *Landmark Cases*. Mark is primed for this project, having also produced an earlier special feature on the Supreme Court's iconic building. For this series, Mark is aided by the editorial team of Tanya Chattman, our Supreme Court producer; videojournalist Adrienne Hoar; and researcher Julia Ishiyama.

C-SPAN is pleased to partner with the Philadelphia-based National Constitution Center for this special television series. The Constitution Center's president and CEO Jeffrey Rosen, who authored the introduction to this book, is one of the country's best-known observers of the Supreme Court. He and members of his senior staff were enormously helpful in the selection of the cases covered, in outreach to the Supreme Court community, and in marketing this project.

As noted, the book in your hands is essentially the professional work of journalist Tony Mauro, a longtime friend to C-SPAN, who has been covering the Court for over thirty-five years. His 2006 edition of *Illustrated Great Decisions of the Supreme Court* has been enormously helpful in C-SPAN's preparation for our television series and we were pleased that he and his publisher, SAGE Publications/CQ Press, gave us permission to excerpt the chapters dealing with the twelve cases in our series to create this special book. Under very tight deadlines, Mr. Mauro graciously helped us bring this book project to press, in particu- lar updating the "Impact" sections to reflect more recent cases. You will find, as we did, that his context for the cases, the interesting stories of the petitioners, and his assessment of the impact of the rulings, are most helpful in setting the stage for the twelve cases highlighted in our series.

Special thanks to C-SPAN's marketing team, under the guidance of vice president Marty Dominguez, for expertly crafting Tony Mauro's text into a well-designed book. Designer Ellen Vest and editor Molly Murchie were leads on the project with assistance from Leslie Rhodes and Rachel Katz. We must also send a shout out to the folks at Offset Paperback Manufacturers for helping us get the manuscript printed at near lightning speed.

In recent years, the Supreme Court has suffered somewhat in public opinion polling. The Court's continuing restrictions on television coverage of its oral arguments prevent C-SPAN from televising the numerous noteworthy cases on its docket for the 2015-16 term. In the interest of informing the public about the Court and its work, our network will continue to offer audio-only coverage of this year's significant arguments. It is also our hope that the *Landmark Cases* series will help inform interested viewers about the Court's long history and about the important effect this institution has had on the development of American society.

Susan Swain
C-SPAN Co-CEO
Washington, D.C.
September 2015

INTRODUCTION

BY JEFFREY ROSEN

President and CEO, National Constitution Center

It's a pleasure to introduce this edition of *Landmark Cases*, a companion
to the C-SPAN television series about twelve historic Supreme Court
decisions, produced in collaboration with the National Constitution
Center. The idea for this exciting series occurred not long ago, at a
National Constitution Center Board of Trustees event in Washington,
D.C. During a public conversation about her remarkable career, Justice
Ruth Bader Ginsburg suggested that it might be useful to focus on the
human stories behind great Supreme Court cases, so that citizens could
connect with the people whose claims about the Constitution have
helped to shape its meaning today. Susan Swain, co-CEO of C-SPAN,
proposed that the network produce a series along the lines that Justice
Ginsburg suggested, and she asked National Constitution Center and
C-SPAN teams to suggest twelve significant cases that might bring the
Constitution to life.

Like C-SPAN, the National Constitution Center is a private
non-profit with an inspiring non-partisan mission. Just as C-SPAN was
created by the cable television industry to provide balanced, unedited
coverage of Congress and other public events, so the National Constitution Center was chartered by Congress "to disseminate information
about the United States Constitution on a non-partisan basis."

With that non-partisan charter firmly in mind, my National Constitution Center colleagues Michael Gerhardt, Scholar in Residence,
and Danieli Evans, Senior Fellow for Constitution Studies, working in
collaboration with the great C-SPAN team, selected the twelve cases
that are the focus of the series and this book. While there are far more
than a dozen cases that are landmarks in the history of constitutional
law, we chose these twelve cases because all of them addressed previously
unanswered constitutional questions, have had enduring impact on
American law and society, are among the most frequently cited by
courts and scholars, and reflect a cross section of the range and diversity
of the constitutional debates that the Court has addressed in the past
two centuries.

The Supreme Court, of course, decides only hard cases, and at the National Constitution Center, we encourage citizens to educate themselves about the best arguments on all sides of any constitutional debate, expressed in majority opinions and in dissents. Many of the cases the Court decides are challenging because they raise open and unresolved constitutional issues that involve hugely important stakes for the parties, whose basic liberties are often in conflict. The cases we've selected dramatically illustrate these constitutional and personal stakes.

Here are examples of the kinds of questions raised by our twelve landmark cases: whether, before the Civil War, a slave named Dred Scott was able to sue for his freedom because he had traveled to free territory, and whether Congress had the authority to outlaw slavery in federal territories; whether the president had the power to order Fred Korematsu, an American of Japanese ancestry, and others like him on the West Coast, to be placed in internment camps for the duration of World War II; whether the federal Constitution limits the authority of police officers to force confessions out of people held in their custody; whether the president, on his own authority, may take control over the nation's steel mills during the Korean war, in order to avert a national strike that could have left Americans abroad without the weapons to protect themselves; and whether young African American children could be barred from attending public schools with white children.

And here are the twelve landmark cases, and the reasons for their significance:

Marbury v. Madison — The first case in which the Supreme Court declared the foundations for its power under the Constitution to decide questions of constitutional law and strike down a federal law as unconstitutional.

Scott v. Sandford — Widely regarded as the Supreme Court's worst decision, the Court ruled that African Americans were not, and could never be, citizens of the United States, and that a federal law purporting to outlaw slavery in federal territories violated the constitutional rights of slave owners to own other people as slaves.

Slaughterhouse Cases — In the first case in which the Supreme Court interpreted the newly ratified Fourteenth Amendment, it nullified and read out of existence its central clause guaranteeing the privileges and immunities of American citizens.

Lochner v. New York — The most important decision in which the Supreme Court held that the Fourteenth Amendment's Due Process Clause guarantees employers a fundamental right to contract, a right which the Court said was violated by a New York law establishing maximum hours for bakers.

Schenck v. New York — In the first major case in which the Supreme Court considered the meaning of the First Amendment, it unanimously upheld the Espionage Act of 1917, which made it a crime for people to distribute leaflets, or otherwise criticize the draft or World War I.

Korematsu v. United States — In spite of its claim that laws based on race require extraordinary justification, the Supreme Court, in a 5-4 decision, upheld the legality of President Roosevelt's executive order confining Japanese Americans on the West Coast to internment camps. Subsequently, President Reagan signed a law that paid the survivors and their families reparations for their internment.

Youngstown Sheet & Tube Co. v. Sawyer — In striking down President Truman's executive order seizing control of the nation's steel mills to avert a national strike that he felt would have crippled American forces in the Korean War, the Court set forth the modern framework on separation of powers under the U.S. Constitution.

Brown v. Board of Education of Topeka — In a decision widely viewed as the most important of the twentieth century, the Court struck down state-mandated segregation of the races in public schools.

Baker v. Carr — For the first time, the Supreme Court held that it had the authority to review the constitutionality of state redistricting laws (attempts to redraw voting districts), ushering in the modern era in which it closely supervises American elections.

Mapp v. Ohio — Revolutionizing criminal procedure, the Supreme Court, for the first time, ruled that even though the Fourth Amendment applies explicitly only to the federal government, the Fourteenth Amendment requires states to comply with its safeguards.

Miranda v. Arizona — In another decision transforming criminal law, the Supreme Court ruled that the Constitution requires the police to inform anyone held in their custody of their constitutional rights to remain silent and receive the assistance of a lawyer.

Roe v. Wade — Holding that the Fourteenth Amendment guaranteed to women the fundamental right to choose whether to terminate their pregnancies, the Court established a framework for balancing a woman's liberty interest against the state's interest in protecting fetal and maternal life.

All of us at the National Constitution Center and C-SPAN hope that you enjoy journalist Tony Mauro's insights in this book, and the *Landmark Cases* series it accompanies. And please learn more about these twelve cases, and about the Supreme Court in general, by reading the full opinions in each of these cases, both the majority decisions and the dissents, with an open mind. After evaluating the best arguments on all sides of the great cases that have helped shaped the U.S. Constitution, you can decide for yourself which arguments persuade you most.

One of the great privileges — and responsibilities — of the American constitutional system is the ability to educate ourselves about what the Constitution says, what the Supreme Court has interpreted it to mean in the past, and what we think it should mean in the future. On behalf of C-SPAN and the National Constitution Center, thank you for joining us in this exciting project of constitutional education.

For more information about the National Constitution Center, visit constitutioncenter.org.

Chief Justice John Marshall, author of the majority opinion.
Source: Library of Congress

MARBURY v. MADISON

Subject:	Separation of powers
Decided:	February 24, 1803
Chief Justice:	John Marshall (F, John Adams appointee)
Petitioner:	William Marbury, federal circuit judicial appointee
Respondent:	James Madison, U.S. secretary of state
Vote:	4-0 for Madison
Majority Opinion:	Chief Justice John Marshall
	5 U.S. 137
	laws.findlaw.com/US/5/137.html

DECISION

The Supreme Court has the power to review acts of Congress and to declare laws unconstitutional and invalid. The Court struck down a law that increased its authority to issue "writs of mandamus," or orders to government officials.

BACKGROUND

In the early days of the Republic, the Supreme Court did not occupy an exalted position in the government. When the capital city was being built, no one thought to create a separate building or even a chamber for the Court's proceedings. Instead, as an afterthought, the Court was assigned to a "meanly furnished" room on the first floor of the Capitol building. This oversight would not be corrected until 1935, when the Supreme Court building was completed.

The Court was so unimportant to the new nation that John Jay, the first chief justice, resigned to become governor of New York, a job he thought more worthwhile. Jay later complained that the Court position lacked "energy, weight, and dignity."

All that would change under John Marshall, who served as chief justice from 1801 to 1835. The vehicle for this change was *Marbury v. Madison*.

Compared with the ultimate importance of the decision in the nation's history, the actual facts of the case were trivial. As Court historian Leo Pfeffer wrote about the case in *This Honorable Court*, "A mighty oak has grown out of a quite insignificant acorn, for as important as the decision in the case may have been, so unimportant was the specific lawsuit which gave rise to it."

The case arose out of the political dispute over the so-called midnight judges, whose commissions were signed by President John Adams on the final night of his administration in 1801. Following Thomas Jefferson's victory over Adams in the election of 1800, Adams's Federalist allies in Congress sought to extend their party's influence by passing legislation that authorized sixteen federal circuit judges and forty-two justices of the peace in Washington, D.C. Congress also reduced the size of the Supreme Court from six to five justices to deprive Jefferson of any quick appointments.

Adams appointed the judges, and the Senate confirmed them. Adams was completing the final paperwork by signing the commissions that would allow the judges to begin work. For reasons still unknown, John Marshall — who was performing the dual tasks of secretary of state and chief justice at the time — failed to deliver the commissions to all of the appointed judges.

William Marbury and three other appointees who did not receive their commissions petitioned the new president's secretary of state, James Madison, to deliver them. But Jefferson, who was thinking of abolishing the new judgeships, told Madison to hold off. The four appointees in limbo went to the Supreme Court to ask that it order Madison to deliver their commissions.

Marshall, whose initial error launched the case, took a central and confrontational role in resolving it as chief justice — a conflict of interest that likely would have caused him to step aside from deciding the case if it occurred today. In December 1801 he ordered the Jefferson administration to respond to Marbury's request at the next session of the Court. The first major test of the power of the Court in relation to the other branches of government was set in motion. The showdown was delayed because Congress, seeking to ward off just such a confrontation, had passed a law putting off the next session of the Court to February 1803, some fourteen months later.

When the Court finally did take up the case, no one appeared to argue on behalf of Madison and the Jefferson administration. Jefferson apparently was content to let the Court rule and deal with the consequences later. The Court took testimony from others, ascertaining that the commissions had been signed but had mysteriously disappeared.

VOTE

4-0, with Chief Justice John Marshall writing the opinion of the Court. Joining him were Justices William Paterson, Bushrod Washington, and Samuel Chase. Justices William Cushing and Alfred Moore did not participate.

HIGHLIGHTS

Chief Justice Marshall faced a dilemma in the case. If he followed his anti-Jefferson inclinations and ordered the commissions delivered to Marbury and the others, Jefferson would almost certainly defy the order, which the Court had no power to enforce. Another possibility was that Jefferson would call for Marshall's impeachment. On the other hand, if the Court dismissed Marbury's plea, it would reaffirm its status as a weakling in the battle among the branches. Marshall, who had probably been weighing his options and even drafting the opinion during the Court's long recess, came up with a third alternative — one that asserted the Court's power in general — but not in this particular case.

The Court first ruled that Marbury and the others were in fact entitled to the commissions that had not been delivered to them. "When the officer is not removable at the will of the executive, the appointment is not revocable, and cannot be annulled. It has conferred legal rights" that cannot be revoked, the Court said.

If Marbury's legal rights had been violated, Marshall asserted, he was entitled to some sort of remedy. "The government of the United States has been emphatically termed a government of laws, and not of men. It will certainly cease to deserve this high appellation, if the laws furnish no remedy for the violation of a vested legal right."

The remedy in this instance is a writ of mandamus, Marshall wrote — just the kind of writ that Marbury sought, and just the kind that Congress had authorized the Court to issue when it established the court system in 1789. But — and this is the crux of the decision — Marshall ruled that Congress did not have the power under the Constitution to give the Court that authority. "The authority, therefore, given to the supreme court by the act establishing the judicial courts of the United States, to issue writs of mandamus to public officers appears not to be warranted by the constitution," Marshall wrote.

Congress, Marshall concluded, cannot act outside the Constitution, and the law that gave the Court mandamus power was unconstitutional. Paradoxically, by ruling that the Court was powerless to help Marbury, the Court was asserting its supreme power to rule acts of Congress unconstitutional.

EXCERPTS

From Chief Justice Marshall's opinion of the Court: "The constitution vests the whole judicial power of the United States in one supreme court, and such inferior courts as congress shall, from time to time, ordain and establish. This power is expressly extended to all cases arising under the laws of the United States; and consequently, in some form, may be exercised over the present case; because the right claimed is given by a law of the United States.... .

"If it had been intended to leave it in the discretion of the legislature to apportion the judicial power between the supreme and inferior courts according to the will of that body, it would certainly have been useless to have proceeded further than to have defined the judicial power, and the tribunals in which it should be vested. The subsequent part of the section is mere surplusage, is entirely without meaning, if such is to be the construction. If congress remains at liberty to give this Court appellate jurisdiction, where the Constitution has declared their jurisdiction shall be original; and original jurisdiction, where the constitution has declared it shall be appellate; the distribution of jurisdiction made in the constitution, is form without substance.... .

"…The constitution is either a superior, paramount law, unchangeable by ordinary means, or it is on a level with ordinary legislative acts, and like other acts, is alterable when the legislature shall please to alter it.

"If the former part of the alternative be true, then a legislative act contrary to the constitution is not law: if the latter part be true, then written constitutions are absurd attempts, on the part of the people, to limit a power in its own nature illimitable… .

"It is emphatically the province and duty of the judicial department to say what the law is. Those who apply the rule to particular cases, must of necessity expound and interpret that rule. If two laws conflict with each other, the courts must decide on the operation of each. So, if a law be in opposition to the constitution: if both the law and the constitution apply to a particular case, so that the court must either decide that case conformably to the law, disregarding the constitution; or conformably to the constitution, disregarding the law: the court must determine which of these conflicting rules governs the case. This is of the very essence of judicial duty."

IMPACT

The Court strikes down acts of Congress rarely, and when it does so, it often emphasizes what a weighty course of action it is. Imagine what it must have been like to do it for the first time. In a young nation where the boundary lines between the branches of government were still uncharted, it was a remarkable — and crucial — assertion of judicial power and independence.

The power of the courts to declare acts of the legislature unconstitutional had its roots in Britain and had been asserted in the *Federalist Papers*. But most scholars think it was essential for the U.S. Supreme Court to state its power explicitly.

The powers of Congress and the president were clear from the start, wrote Court scholar Alexander Bickel, but "the institution of the judiciary needed to be summoned up out of the constitutional vapors, shaped and maintained; and the great chief justice, John Marshall — not single-handed, but first and foremost — was there to do it and did."

Historian Charles Warren called *Marbury v. Madison* "the fundamental decision in the American system of constitutional law." Court scholar Bernard Schwartz said the decision is the "*sine qua non* of the

American constitutional machinery: draw out this particular bolt, and the machinery falls to pieces."

The decision was not immediately recognized as a landmark, however. Initial press reports focused on the political aspects of the showdown between Jefferson and Marshall. And it took more than 60 years before the Court again struck down an act of Congress. After that, Supreme Court rejection of acts of Congress became less unusual. More than 160 laws have been declared unconstitutional in whole or in part by the Supreme Court — ranging from the Missouri Compromise to the federal income tax to the Defense of Marriage Act.

The ruling was notable for another reason. In the Court's earliest days, it was common for justices to write individual opinions in each case. Marshall decided that the Court should speak with one voice, so *Marbury v. Madison* was written as the single opinion for the entire Court. Justices could still write concurring or dissenting opinions, but one writing stood as the decision of the Court. In 1999 Justice Stephen Breyer raised eyebrows by using the pronoun "I" in a majority opinion, rather than "we." Breyer later offered assurances in correspondence with law professors that the usage was inadvertent and did not represent a break with the Marshall tradition.

In recent years a slow-simmering debate over the wisdom of *Marbury* had taken place in political and academic circles, though it appears unlikely that such a bedrock precedent would be upended anytime soon.

Both liberals and conservatives have questioned the wisdom of *Marbury's* grant of the power of judicial review to the Supreme Court. In the early 1980s Edwin Meese III, attorney general in the Reagan administration, said the executive branch should not necessarily feel bound by Supreme Court rulings interpreting the meaning of laws. More recently some liberal scholars, including Harvard University's Mark Tushnet, have argued that judicial review has yielded bad results as often as good ones and is antidemocratic. And, some Republican candidates for president in 2016 have suggested the Court should not have the final word.

SCOTT v. SANDFORD

Subject:	Slavery
Decided:	March 6, 1857
Chief Justice:	Roger B. Taney (D, Jackson appointee)
Petitioner:	Dred Scott, Missouri slave
Respondent:	John Sanford, slave owner's agent
Vote:	7-2 for Sanford
Majority Opinion:	Chief Justice Roger B. Taney
	60 U.S. 393
	laws.findlaw.com/US/60/393.html

DECISION

Under the Constitution, blacks are not citizens of the United States and may not become citizens. Because they are not citizens, they may not file suit in federal courts. Congress does not have the authority to prohibit slavery in the territories. As a result the Missouri Compromise, which outlawed slavery in parts of the Louisiana Territory, is unconstitutional. Slaves who were moved to territories where slavery had been outlawed were not automatically freed.

BACKGROUND

Before the Civil War, the status of slavery in the new parts of the growing nation was a subject of fervent debate between supporters of slavery and those who wanted to abolish it. Congressional efforts to limit slavery in the territories divided the institution for decades. The newly created Republican Party was devoted to preventing the spread of slavery. In this charged climate, it was perhaps inevitable that both sides would look for a judicial solution. The chance to come up with such a remedy arose in the case of Dred Scott.

Born in Virginia, Scott was sold as a slave to John Emerson, a St. Louis physician. Emerson took Scott along when he joined the military, and in various postings Scott was taken to Illinois, a free state, and to the Wisconsin Territory, which was also free. While in the Wisconsin

Missouri slave Dred Scott.
Source: Library of Congress

Territory, Scott married another slave, Harriet Robinson. During a tour in Louisiana, Emerson married Irene Sanford. When Emerson was transferred to Florida, his wife and the Scotts returned to St. Louis. Dr. Emerson died in 1843, after which the Scotts continued to work for his widow and for her brother, John Sanford of New York.

In 1846 the Scotts sued for their freedom, claiming that they had been emancipated when Emerson took them to the slave-free zones of Illinois and the Wisconsin Territory. Their claim, which was consolidated under Dred Scott's name, was supported by the prevailing legal theory in Missouri at the time, which was, "once free, always free." After lengthy delays, the Scotts won at trial, but the state Supreme Court ruled against them. By now, the case had become well known, and the Missouri Supreme Court may have felt compelled to protect state traditions against outside antislavery influences. The court ruled that in Missouri Scott was still a slave.

Scott's lawyers wanted to appeal the case to the U.S. Supreme Court. For legal and strategic reasons, the best way to do so was to name an out-of-state person as the defendant, thereby triggering federal court jurisdiction over legal disputes between citizens of different states. They chose John Sanford, who was acting as his sister's agent in the litigation anyway. To complete the requirements for federal court jurisdiction, Scott claimed he was a Missouri citizen. The case became known as *Scott v. Sandford* because Sanford's name was misspelled in the records.

A federal trial judge in 1854 agreed with Missouri's high court, finding that Scott was still a slave under Missouri law. The judge also found that Scott was not a citizen of any state, so he could not trigger federal court jurisdiction.

As the case moved to the U.S. Supreme Court, the legal stakes rose and it became a platform for the broader national debate over slavery. Sanford's lawyers argued for the first time that the Missouri Compromise, which had made the Wisconsin Territory slave free, was unconstitutional and therefore did not have the effect of emancipating Scott. They also questioned whether Scott was a citizen and had any right to sue in federal court.

Reflecting the complexity and tension in the case, the Supreme Court heard arguments in it twice, both in February and December of 1856. The outcome was probably not in doubt: Five of the nine justices on the Court were southerners, several from slaveholding families.

Chief Justice Taney, nearly eighty years old, was a Marylander already on record in support of slavery.

Still, there was a considerable amount of behind-the-scenes maneuvering over the case. At first most justices wanted to issue a limited ruling that would avoid the issue of the Missouri Compromise — a law Congress had already repealed with the Kansas-Nebraska Act of 1854, which declared congressional neutrality on the extension of slavery. Instead, these justices would rely on Missouri state law to find that Scott was still a slave. But when two justices said they would dissent and vote to strike down the Missouri Compromise, the rest of the Court agreed the issue needed to be resolved. According to Chief Justice William Rehnquist in a 1998 book, the justices opposing the Missouri Compromise even enlisted President-elect James Buchanan to lobby Justice Robert Grier, a fellow Pennsylvanian, in their effort. Buchanan agreed, and Grier joined the majority. "These machinations, of course, were grossly inappropriate," Rehnquist wrote.

Finally on March 6, 1857, eleven years after Scott first sued, and two days after the inauguration of President Buchanan, the Court was ready to rule.

VOTE

7-2, with Chief Justice Roger B. Taney writing for the Court. He was joined by Justices James M. Wayne, John Catron, Peter V. Daniel, Samuel Nelson, Robert C. Grier, and John A. Campbell. Dissenting were Justices John McLean and Benjamin R. Curtis.

HIGHLIGHTS

The nearly 250 pages of the Court's decision, with separate opinions from all nine justices, are not a model of clarity. Scholars have even debated about which of the justices' writings actually represents the decision of the Court.

It is now generally agreed that Chief Justice Taney's opinion, even though it has been attacked for flawed reasoning and an inaccurate statement of facts, speaks for the Court. Taney's opinion is grounded in his view of the "original intent" of the Framers, namely what the Framers had in mind about slaves and what the status of slaves was at the time of the drafting of the Constitution.

"They were at that time considered as a subordinate and inferior class of beings, who had been subjugated by the dominant race, and, whether emancipated or not, yet remained subject to their authority, and had no rights or privileges but such as those who held the power and the Government might choose to grant them," Taney wrote. It was a view of the world that presumed that blacks had no basic natural rights as human beings and that the only rights they could have were those enacted by government. From this perspective, Dred Scott could not be viewed as a citizen of the United States.

Taney acknowledged that the Declaration of Independence declares that "all men are created equal." But, he goes on, "The general words above quoted would seem to embrace the whole human family, and if they were used in a similar instrument at this day would be so understood. But it is too clear for dispute, that the enslaved African race were not intended to be included."

Contrast this view with Justice Curtis's dissent: "Slavery, being contrary to natural right, is created only by municipal law. This is not only plain in itself, and agreed by all writers on the subject, but is inferable from the Constitution and has been explicitly declared by this Court." In other words, Curtis believed that under the laws of nature all human beings have basic rights. Slavery exists only because of laws that are passed in contradiction to those rights, Curtis said, a view of human rights completely opposite from Taney's.

But Taney's view enabled him and the justices in the majority to absolve themselves of responsibility for slavery. That belonged to the legislative bodies that can grant and take away the few rights that slaves are given. Taney wrote, "It is not the province of the court to decide upon the justice or injustice, the policy or impolicy, of these laws. The decision of that question belonged to the political or law-making power, to those who formed the sovereignty and framed the Constitution. The duty of the court is to interpret the instrument they have framed with the best lights we can obtain on the subject, and to administer it as we find it, according to its true intent and meaning when it was adopted."

Taney's assertion also led to one of the Court's main conclusions: Because blacks were not citizens at the time of the framing of the Constitution, they were not entitled to sue in federal courts. So Dred Scott was asking the federal courts to do something they had no jurisdiction to do. Taney also insisted that the Framers of the Constitution viewed slaves as property, not people. "The right of property in a slave is distinctly and expressly affirmed in the Constitution," he wrote.

The next step was for Taney to rule that the Constitution gave Congress no power to enact legislation affecting the territories — certainly not legislation as sweeping as the Missouri Compromise. Taney reached that conclusion by a very narrow and much-disputed reading of the Constitution's provision on territories. So Scott had lost on another score: he could not be free now if he had never been in a free state. Because the Missouri Compromise was illegitimate, Scott's travels to the Wisconsin Territory and to Illinois did not turn him into a free man.

In dissent, Justice Curtis also sharply disputed Taney's version of history at the time of the framing of the Constitution. "To determine whether any free persons, descended from Africans held in slavery, were citizens of the United States under the Confederation, and consequently at the time of the adoption of the Constitution of the United States, it is only necessary to know whether any such persons were citizens of either of the States under the Confederation at the time of the adoption of the Constitution. Of this there can be no doubt," Curtis wrote.

Curtis eloquently attacked the Court majority for basing its decision on an inaccurate view of history and the meaning of the Constitution. "When a strict interpretation of the Constitution, according to the fixed rules which govern the interpretation of laws, is abandoned, and the theoretical opinions of individuals are allowed to control its meaning, we have no longer a Constitution; we are under the government of individual men who for the time being have power to declare what the Constitution is, according to their own views of what it ought to mean."

Justice McLean also dissented, arguing that Scott had rights as a citizen. "Being born under our Constitution and laws, no naturalization is required, as one of foreign birth, to make him a citizen. The most general and appropriate definition of the term citizen is 'a freeman.' Being a freeman, and having his domicil [*sic*] in a State different from that of the defendant, he is a citizen within the act of Congress, and the courts of the Union are open to him."

EXCERPTS

From Chief Taney's majority opinion: "The question before us is, whether the class of persons described in the plea in abatement compose a portion of this people, and are constituent members of this sovereignty? We think they are not, and that they are not included, and were not intended to be included, under the word 'citizens' in the Constitution, and can therefore claim none of the rights and privileges which that instrument provides for and secures to citizens of the United States.... .

"In the opinion of the court, the legislation and histories of the times, and the language used in the Declaration of Independence, show, that neither the class of persons who had been imported as slaves, nor their descendants, whether they had become free or not, were then acknowledged as a part of the people, nor intended to be included in the general words used in that memorable instrument.... .

"... [T]he right of property in a slave is distinctly and expressly affirmed in the Constitution. The right to traffic in it, like an ordinary article of merchandise and property, was guarantied [*sic*] to the citizens of the United States, in every State that might desire it, for twenty years.... .

"... [I]t is the opinion of the Court that the act of Congress which prohibited a citizen from holding and owning property of this kind in the territory of the United States north of the line therein mentioned, is not warranted by the Constitution, and is therefore void; and that neither Dred Scott himself, nor any of his family, were made free by being carried into this territory, even if they had been carried there by the owner, with the intention of becoming a permanent resident."

IMPACT

It would probably overstate the case to say that the Dred Scott decision triggered the Civil War, but historians agree that it was certainly a contributing factor. The decision made it clear that there would be no easy way, certainly no judicial way, to end slavery or to confine it to the southern states. The Court had declared slavery to be a national institution that Congress could not prohibit in the territories, which represented the future of a growing nation. With no easy end to the strife over slavery in sight, war between North and South became more likely.

Reaction to the ruling was explosive. Abolitionist Horace Greeley's *New York Tribune* said the decision "is entitled to just so much moral weight as would be the judgment of those congregated in any Washington bar room." A Georgia newspaper, on the other hand, boasted that "southern opinion on the subject of southern slavery is now the supreme law of the land."

The decision also was a frequent theme for discussion in the famed Lincoln-Douglas debates that preceded the 1858 Illinois Senate race. Abraham Lincoln said the Supreme Court had been enlisted in a conspiracy to "nationalize slavery," while Stephen Douglas accused Lincoln of declaring war on the Supreme Court. In Lincoln's first inaugural address, delivered moments after Chief Justice Taney swore him in, Lincoln was likely referring to the Dred Scott decision when he said "the people will have ceased to be their own rulers" if the Supreme Court can set national policy.

Decades after the Dred Scott decision, Chief Justice Charles Evans Hughes called it the Supreme Court's greatest "self-inflicted wound." The decision's dogged support of slavery earned it the first place position in Court scholar Bernard Schwartz's list of worst Supreme Court decisions in history. "No decision in our history has done more to injure the reputation of the Court," wrote Schwartz.

Scott v. Sandford was overturned, not by the Court but through the constitutional amendment process. The Thirteenth Amendment, ratified in 1865, abolished slavery altogether, and the Fourteenth Amendment, ratified in 1868, guaranteed citizenship to all persons born or naturalized in the United States, regardless of race or prior servitude.

As a result, in spite of its explosive political impact, the decision had relatively little legal importance, with one exception. Writing on the Missouri Compromise, historian Don Fehrenbacher said, "This was the first instance in which a major federal law was ruled unconstitutional. The decision is therefore a landmark in the development of judicial review and in the growth of judicial power."

SLAUGHTERHOUSE CASES

*The Butchers' Benevolent Association of New Orleans v.
The Crescent City Livestock Landing and Slaughterhouse Co.*

Esteben v. Louisiana

Subject:	Federal and state citizenship rights
Decided:	April 14, 1873
Chief Justice:	Salmon P. Chase (R, Lincoln appointee)
Petitioner:	Louisiana butchers shut out of a government-regulated slaughterhouse monopoly
Respondent:	Butchers accused of having a monopoly on Louisiana slaughterhouses, and the government regulating the monopoly
Vote:	5-4 for the government-regulated monopoly
Majority Opinion:	Justice Samuel F. Miller
	83 U.S. 36
	laws.findlaw.com/US/83/36.html

DECISION

The Privileges or Immunities Clause of the Fourteenth Amendment does not protect the right to labor. Therefore, a state is not in violation of the Fourteenth Amendment if it grants monopolies to businesses. The Fourteenth Amendment's Due Process Clause also does not guarantee the right to carry on a business.

BACKGROUND

The post-Civil War amendments to the Constitution — the Thirteenth, Fourteenth, and Fifteenth Amendments — were adopted primarily to end slavery and its oppressive effects on black Americans. It was ironic, then, that the first major Supreme Court case testing the meaning of those amendments involved not former slaves but white Louisiana businessmen.

The Reconstruction "carpetbag" legislature of Louisiana passed a law in 1869 that gave one company the exclusive right to operate a meat slaughterhouse in the city. In the days before modern refrigeration and sanitation, this government-regulated monopoly was to promote public health and reduce the dumping of animal waste into the Mississippi River. Opponents of the law charged that legislators had been bribed by wealthy businessmen to give the monopoly to the Crescent City Livestock Landing and Slaughterhouse Company.

Competing butchers also objected to the law, which forced them to use the government slaughterhouse and to pay for the privilege of doing so. They sued to challenge the law. One of their lawyers was John Campbell, a former U.S. Supreme Court justice from Alabama. Despite his moderate views on slavery, Campbell had resigned his seat when his state seceded from the Union. In addition to a range of other legal arguments, Campbell argued that the law violated the new Fourteenth Amendment to the Constitution. The right of the butchers to do business, he claimed, was one of the "privileges or immunities" of citizenship that the amendment protected.

In his capacity as a circuit judge, Justice Joseph Bradley agreed with Campbell that the Louisiana law violated the Fourteenth Amendment. The amendment gave the federal government the power to protect basic rights at the state level, including the right to labor, he said. His ruling was appealed to the Supreme Court. Three lawsuits involving the Louisiana law (two of which had the same name) were consolidated before the Court and became known, collectively, as the *Slaughterhouse Cases*.

VOTE

5-4, with Justice Samuel F. Miller writing the majority opinion. Joining him were Justices Nathan Clifford, David Davis, William Strong, and

Ward Hunt. Dissenting were Chief Justice Salmon P. Chase and Justices Stephen J. Field, Joseph P. Bradley, and Noah H. Swayne.

HIGHLIGHTS

The part of the Fourteenth Amendment at issue in the case says, "No State shall make or enforce any law which shall abridge the privileges or immunities of citizens of the United States." Some historians say the writers of the Fourteenth Amendment clearly intended these words to make the federal Bill of Rights binding on the states. At the very least, some scholars say, the sponsors of the Fourteenth Amendment wanted to establish one citizenship enjoyed by both blacks and whites and protected by the federal Constitution. The amendment had been passed to counteract the Supreme Court's decision in *Scott v. Sandford*, which was based in part on the notion that U.S. citizenship was distinct from state citizenship.

But in the *Slaughterhouse* decision, Justice Miller and the majority of the Court ruled in a way that maintained the distinction between state and national citizenship and protected only the limited "privileges or immunities" of national citizenship. The rights of state citizens — far broader and more basic — would be interpreted and protected at the state level, without federal intervention.

The Fourteenth Amendment, according to the Court, gave the federal government a very limited role in protecting most of the individual rights people enjoy. To interpret the Fourteenth Amendment otherwise, Miller said, would be "to fetter and degrade the State governments by subjecting them to the control of Congress, in the exercise of powers heretofore universally conceded to them of the most ordinary and fundamental character," and would also radically change "the whole theory of the relations of the State and Federal governments to each other and of both these governments to the people."

Miller did not define what the rights of national citizenship were; that task, he said, would await a future case. But, as examples, he said the Fourteenth Amendment would protect the right of a U.S. citizen to travel to Washington, D.C., and to use navigable waters of the United States.

Apart from these kinds of rights, the Court said the main purpose of the Fourteenth Amendment was to prohibit state laws that discriminated against emancipated slaves. Under Section 5 of the Fourteenth

Amendment, the Court said, Congress was authorized to enact laws to enforce that mandate.

"We doubt very much whether any action of a State not directed by way of discrimination against the Negroes as a class, or on account of their race, will ever be held to come within the purview of this provision," Miller wrote. Under Miller's analysis of the Fourteenth Amendment, the Louisiana law could not be overturned by the Supreme Court or by any part of the federal government. Unless it had to do with the rights of blacks or the limited privileges of national citizenship, a state's action did not bring the Fourteenth Amendment into play.

The dissenting justices sharply disagreed. Justice Field said the case presents an issue "of the gravest importance not merely to the parties here, but to the whole country. It is nothing less than the question whether the recent amendments to the Federal Constitution protect the citizens of the United States against the deprivation of their common rights by State legislation. In my judgment, the fourteenth amendment does afford such protection, and was so intended by the Congress which framed and the States which adopted it." If the Fourteenth Amendment had only the limited meaning that the majority attached to it, Field said, "it was a vain and idle enactment, which accomplished nothing."

Justice Bradley also wrote a dissent, asserting that national citizenship was primary and state citizenship secondary, in the constitutional scheme bolstered by the Fourteenth Amendment. Among the privileges protected by the amendment, said Bradley, is the right to "choose one's calling," which the Louisiana slaughterhouse monopoly law infringed. Bradley added, "To say that these rights and immunities attach only to State citizenship, and not to citizenship of the United States, appears to me to evince a very narrow and insufficient estimate of constitutional history and the rights of men, not to say the rights of the American people."

EXCERPTS

From Justice Miller's majority opinion: "The most cursory glance at these articles discloses a unity of purpose, when taken in connection with the history of the times, which cannot fail to have an important bearing on any question of doubt concerning their true meaning. Nor can such doubts, when any reasonably exist, be safely and rationally solved without a reference to that history, for in it is found the occasion and the necessity for recurring again to the great source of power in this country, the people of the States, for additional guarantees of human rights; additional powers to the Federal government; additional restraints upon those of the States.

"…Under the pressure of all the excited feeling growing out of the war, our statesmen have still believed that the existence of the State with powers for domestic and local government, including the regulation of civil rights — the rights of person and of property — was essential to the perfect working of our complex form of government, though they have thought proper to impose additional limitations on the States, and to confer additional power on that of the Nation.

"But whatever fluctuations may be seen in the history of public opinion on this subject during the period of our national existence, we think it will be found that this court, so far as its functions required, has always held with a steady and an even hand the balance between State and Federal power, and we trust that such may continue to be the history of its relation to that subject so long as it shall have duties to perform which demand of it a construction of the Constitution, or of any of its parts."

IMPACT

Today the distinction between state and federal citizenship has little practical meaning. But at the time of the *Slaughterhouse Cases*, the difference was important. The Court's controversial decision went a long way toward reassuring states' rights supporters that state citizenship still meant something.

The immediate meaning of the decision was, as Court scholar Bernard Schwartz has said, that the recently enacted Privileges or Immunities Clause of the Fourteenth Amendment was "all but read out of the amendment" just a few short years later. An important tool that could have accelerated the protection of individual rights at the state as well as federal level was rendered useless. In Justice Swayne's evocative phrase, the majority opinion turned "what was meant for bread into a stone." It took decades for the Court, in piecemeal fashion, to extend the reach of the Bill of Rights to the states, and it had to use other provisions of the Fourteenth Amendment to do it.

The *Slaughterhouse* decision had considerable impact on civil rights as well. Michael Kent Curtis, author of *No State Shall Abridge*, a book on the Fourteenth Amendment, says that even though the majority said the amendment was meant to protect blacks, it soon was cited "to justify decisions denying them a wide range of rights." The *Slaughterhouse* decision gave energy to states' rights, which as the years went by became a vehicle for Jim Crow laws and statutes that ignored the Bill of Rights.

In Supreme Court jurisprudence, the Privileges or Immunities Clause was largely ignored for more than 125 years. Scholars occasionally expressed renewed interest in it as the source for some new or old right. Suddenly, in a 1999 decision for the Court, Justice John Paul Stevens invoked the clause and triggered new debate over the *Slaughterhouse* decision. In *Saenz v. Roe* Stevens cited the Privileges or Immunities Clause in support of his view that California could not give a different level of welfare benefits to newcomers to the state.

The Court said the right of a newly arrived citizen to enjoy the same privilege or immunities of other citizens of the state was clearly protected by the Fourteenth Amendment, "despite fundamentally differing views concerning the coverage of the privileges or immunities clause of the Fourteenth Amendment, most notably expressed in the majority and dissenting opinions in the *Slaughterhouse Cases*."

Justice Clarence Thomas, who dissented in *Saenz*, said the demise of the clause was responsible for the "disarray" in the Court's Fourteenth Amendment decisions. "I would be open to reevaluating its meaning in an appropriate case," Thomas said, but the *Saenz* case was not the one. In a footnote Thomas also said, "Legal scholars agree on little beyond the conclusion that the clause does not mean what the Court said it meant in 1873."

Some of those scholars reacted positively to the *Saenz* decision, expressing hope that it would result in a revival of the Privileges or Immunities Clause.

That revival has not taken place to any great degree, though Thomas attempted to breathe new life into it again in the 2010 decision *McDonald v. Chicago*. That ruling said the Second Amendment right to bear arms protected individuals against state as well as federal restrictions on firearm use. In a lengthy concurrence, Thomas asserted that the Privileges or Immunities Clause is a "more straightforward path" to applying constitutional rights to states than other sections of the Fourteenth Amendment, such as the Due Process Clause.

Thomas's opinion led constitutional scholar Randy Barnett to proclaim, "Today, the Privileges or Immunities Clause has risen from the grave," though he acknowledged it could take years before the clause is cited widely.

Justice Samuel F. Miller, author of the majority opinion.
Source: Library of Congress

Justice Rufus W. Peckham, author of the majority opinion.
Source: Library of Congress

LOCHNER v. NEW YORK

Subject:	Labor laws
Decided:	April 17, 1905
Chief Justice:	Melville W. Fuller (D, Cleveland appointee)
Petitioner:	Joseph Lochner, Utica, New York, bakery owner
Respondent:	State of New York
Vote:	5-4 for Lochner
Majority Opinion:	Justice Rufus W. Peckham
	198 U.S. 45
	laws.findlaw.com/US/198/45.html

DECISION

A New York law limiting the number of hours a bakery worker can be required to work interferes with the Fourteenth Amendment right of businesses and employees to enter into contracts to buy and sell labor. The justices declared that baking is not an unhealthy trade and that the law limiting hours cannot be justified as a legitimate exercise of police powers to protect health and safety.

BACKGROUND

In many large cities at the turn of the twentieth century, the business of baking bread had little to do with home and hearth. It was a grimy, gritty business conducted mainly in the cellars of tenement buildings because their cramped apartments usually were too small to have ovens of their own. The bakers worked extremely long hours, and, because the workplaces were poorly ventilated, the bakers were exposed to flour dust and fumes as well as intense heat. Conditions were often unsanitary; many workers slept, ate, and washed in the same area where bread was prepared. Muckraking journalists and social reformers attempted to expose these conditions. One New York newspaper ran an article in 1894 headlined "Bread and Filth Cooked Together."

At the same time, the labor movement was becoming increasingly militant on the issue of long working hours, not just in bakeries but in many businesses where twelve- or fourteen-hour days, six or seven days a week, were common. The Haymarket riots in Chicago in 1886 had been triggered by a general strike aimed at generating support for eight-hour workdays. Limiting the number of working hours for laborers was pushed not only as a social benefit, but also as a way to generate new jobs and spread employment around more evenly.

In 1895 the New York legislature responded to the reform movement by passing the Bakeshop Act, which said no bakery employees should be "required or permitted" to work more than ten hours per day or sixty hours per week. Unlike similar laws in other states, New York's carried with it criminal penalties.

In April 1901 a Utica bakery owner named Joseph Lochner was accused of violating the law by forcing one of his workers, Aman Schmitter, to work for more than sixty hours a week. Lochner offered no defense except to attack the law, and he was fined $50 in early 1902. Lochner fought the conviction, but the New York appeals courts upheld the conviction and the law.

Lochner's appeal reached the Supreme Court at an opportune time for him. The Court had begun to take the view that the Fourteenth Amendment protected an individual's right to make contracts. More important, the Court was beginning to view the amendment's guarantee of "due process" as not just a right to fair procedure but to substantive fairness — in this context, a limit on states' power to enact laws that interfered with property and contracts.

VOTE

5-4, with Justice Rufus W. Peckham writing the majority opinion. Joining him were Chief Justice Melville W. Fuller and Justices David J. Brewer, Henry B. Brown, and Joseph McKenna. Justices John Marshall Harlan, Edward D. White, William R. Day, and Oliver Wendell Holmes Jr. dissented.

HIGHLIGHTS

The Court divided sharply over the constitutionality of the New York law. According to historian Paul Kens's 1998 book on the case, rumor had it that Peckham's majority opinion started out as a dissent. Sometimes a dissenting argument can be so convincing that justices in the majority change their minds, turning the opinion on its head.

To strike down the Bakeshop Act, the Court first had to decide that the law was not a legitimate exercise of the state's police power, which had been defined over the years to include government's interest in protecting the health, safety, and morals of society.

In a section of the opinion that has been criticized for ignoring the realities of the working world, the Court said baking was not an unhealthy profession. "The trade of a baker, in and of itself, is not an unhealthy one to that degree which would authorize the legislature to interfere with the right to labor, and with the right of free contract on the part of the individual, either as employer or employee."

As a result, the Court concluded that the New York law had nothing to do with the general health of the public. "Viewed in the light of a purely labor law, with no reference whatever to the question of health, we think that a law like the one before us involves neither the safety, the morals, nor the welfare, of the public, and that the interest of the public is not in the slightest degree affected by such an act."

If the law was not intended to protect workers' health, what then was its purpose? The Court concluded, "It seems to us that the real object and purpose were simply to regulate the hours of labor between the master and his employees … in a private business.… . Under such circumstances, the freedom of master and employee to contract with each other in relation to their employment, and in defining the same, cannot be prohibited or interfered with without violating the Federal Constitution."

Two forceful dissents make clear how divided the Court was. Harlan said the Court should not have given such short shrift to the motives of the New York legislature. "The rule is universal that a legislative enactment, Federal or state, is never to be disregarded or held invalid unless it be, beyond question, plainly and palpably in excess of legislative power."

Holmes's dissent asserted that government interferes with personal liberties in a variety of ways that are constitutional. "The liberty of the citizen to do as he likes so long as he does not interfere with the liberty of others to do the same, which has been a shibboleth for some well-known writers, is interfered with by school laws, by the Post Office, by every state or municipal institution which takes his money for purposes thought desirable, whether he likes it or not."

Holmes added, "The Fourteenth Amendment does not enact Mr. Herbert Spencer's Social Statics." This was a sarcastic reference to the social Darwinism of economist Spencer, whose views Holmes had summarized. Spencer believed the primary role of government was merely to make sure that individual liberties were not interfered with any more than necessary. Holmes was concerned that Spencer's "laissez-faire" view of government had just been written into constitutional law.

EXCERPTS

From Justice Peckham's majority opinion: "The general right to make a contract in relation to his business is part of the liberty of the individual protected by the 14th Amendment of the Federal Constitution. Under that provision no state can deprive any person of life, liberty, or property without due process of law. The right to purchase or to sell labor is part of the liberty protected by this amendment, unless there are circumstances which exclude the right. There are, however, certain powers, existing in the sovereignty of each state in the Union, somewhat vaguely termed police powers, the exact description and limitation of which have not been attempted by the courts. Those powers, broadly stated, and without, at present, any attempt at a more specific limitation, relate to the safety, health, morals, and general welfare of the public. Both property and liberty are held on such reasonable conditions as may be imposed by the governing power of the State in the exercise of those powers, and with such conditions the 14th Amendment was not designed to interfere."

IMPACT

Lochner v. New York is the only Supreme Court decision that has given
its name to an era. The *"Lochner* Era" was a 32-year period in which the
Supreme Court and other courts cited the case to strike down a large
number of legislative efforts to reform economic conditions through
regulations on business. Laws setting minimum wages and prohibiting
child labor were invalidated in the name of *Lochner*. A lawyer for the
bakery workers said flatly that the *Lochner* decision meant "Everything
that furthers the interests of employers is constitutional." Union bakers
eventually won shorter working days through collective bargaining.

In a 1910 speech President Theodore Roosevelt — who, as a New
York legislator had introduced a bill to regulate the cigar industry —
referred to the *Lochner* decision by name as an example of the Supreme
Court frustrating popular will. The Court, Roosevelt said, had placed
"altogether insurmountable obstacles in the path of needed social reforms."
Some recent commentators have said the impact of the decision was
more limited, noting that some laws restricting business, especially laws
that cited public health and safety, were upheld. In the 1917 decision
Bunting v. Oregon, for example, the Court upheld an Oregon law establishing a ten-hour workday for industrial workers.

Lochner's force continued to be felt in the early days of President
Franklin Roosevelt's New Deal legislation. A conservative bloc on the
Court helped strike down several pieces of New Deal legislation that
regulated businesses, although *Lochner* was not specifically cited.

Gradually, however, the perspective of the Court shifted, and in 1937
the Court effectively buried *Lochner*. In *West Coast Hotel v. Parrish*, in
which the Court upheld a state law setting a minimum wage for workers, the majority said, "The Constitution does not speak of freedom of
contract." It also adopted a more expansive view of the power of states
to regulate businesses. "In dealing with the relation of employer and employed, the legislature has necessarily a wide field of discretion in order
that there may be suitable protection of health and safety, and that peace
and good order may be promoted through regulations designed to insure
wholesome conditions of work and freedom from oppression."

Echoes of the debate over the *Lochner* decision, however, are still
heard today. It is criticized not only because of its effect on reform legislation but also because it seems to many to be case of judicial activism

— imposing an economic theory favored by the Court's majority on the rest of the country, contrary to the expressed view of elected legislators.

In that vein, the ruling cropped up in the 2015 Supreme Court decision requiring that states allow same-sex marriage, *Obergefell v. Hodges*. Chief Justice John Roberts Jr. dissented and invoked *Lochner* as an example of the court's occasional "error of converting personal preferences into constitutional mandates."

Conservative justices have revisited the concept of economic rights, but in the context of the Fifth Amendment rather than the Fourteenth. In *Nollan v. California Coastal Commission* in 1987, *Lucas v. South Carolina Coastal Council* in 1992, and *Dolan v. City of Tigard* in 1994, the Court gave greater recognition to the takings clause of the Fifth Amendment. That clause prohibits government from taking private property without compensation.

In a 2015 speech Rand Paul, a libertarian senator from Kentucky and a 2016 Republican presidential candidate, called *Lochner* "a wonderful decision" because it protected the right to make contracts against government regulation.

So, as Kens wrote in his book on the case, "*Lochner* is not dead."

SCHENCK v. UNITED STATES

Subject:	Freedom of speech
Decided:	March 3, 1919
Chief Justice:	Edward D. White (R, Taft appointee)
Petitioner:	Charles Schenck, general secretary of Philadelphia's Socialist Party
Respondent:	United States government
Vote:	9-0 for United States government
Majority Opinion:	Justice Oliver Wendell Holmes Jr.
	249 U.S. 47
	laws.findlaw.com/US/249/47.html

DECISION

The Espionage Act of 1917, which bars acts of insubordination and interference with military recruitment, is constitutional, even when it is used to punish speech that would be permissible in times of peace. The First Amendment is not absolute, and freedom of speech may be restricted when the expression poses a "clear and present danger" to values that Congress is entitled to protect.

BACKGROUND

Before the declaration of war in 1917, the idea of sending U.S. troops to fight the Germans and save the British was not popular with the American people. However, once Congress declared war, there was considerable pressure to stifle dissent about the war. Elihu Root, one of

Justice Oliver Wendell Holmes Jr., author of the majority opinion in the unanimous vote.
Source: Harvard Law School Library

President Woodrow Wilson's advisers, said in early 1917, "We must have no criticism now."

Police surveillance increased, and Americans were encouraged to report their neighbors' "disloyal" acts. Congress enacted the Espionage Act of 1917, which made acts of insubordination and disloyalty punishable by prison terms of up to twenty years. It was the first time since the Alien and Sedition Acts early in the nation's history that criticism of government had been criminalized. Sponsors said that tolerating disloyal public statements might undermine efforts to draft and recruit young people into military service. More than 2,000 people were prosecuted under the act.

One of them was Charles Schenck, general secretary of Philadelphia's Socialist Party. In 1917 the party directed Schenck to prepare a leaflet that would be distributed to young men conscripted in the recently enacted military draft.

The party printed 15,000 copies of Schenck's leaflet, which compared conscription to slavery. It encouraged readers to sign a petition urging Congress to repeal the draft law but did not explicitly tell recipients to resist the draft. After some of the leaflets were mailed, federal officials arrested Schenck and other party officials under the Espionage Act. Schenck was tried, found guilty, and sentenced to six months in jail. His appeal went directly to the Supreme Court because it amounted to a challenge to the constitutionality of a federal law, which the Court could consider without prior review by an appeals court. It fell to Justice Oliver Wendell Holmes Jr. to write the Court's opinion.

The revered Justice Holmes had already given some thought to the Espionage Act. In the summer of 1918, he had a chance encounter with Judge Learned Hand, a federal district court judge who had recently ruled in favor of a magazine called *The Masses* in an Espionage Act case. The two discussed free speech issues and corresponded afterwards. Hand wrote to Holmes, "We must be tolerant of opposite opinions." Holmes replied that freedom of speech was no different from "freedom from vaccination" and could be restricted by a majority.

The exchange did not bode well for Schenck's chances before the justices, who were not immune to the general call for patriotism in wartime. As historian Peter Irons put it in the book *A People's History of the Supreme Court*, "In a symbolic but very real sense, the justices hung up their black robes and donned the khaki uniforms of American soldiers."

VOTE

9-0, with Justice Oliver Wendell Holmes Jr. writing for the majority. Joining him were Chief Justice Edward D. White and Justices Joseph McKenna, William R. Day, Willis Van Devanter, Mahlon Pitney, James C. McReynolds, Louis D. Brandeis, and John H. Clarke.

HIGHLIGHTS

Justice Holmes's opinion is brief and direct. It deals with the First Amendment issue in just two paragraphs, which have lived on in importance.

The opinion starts by describing, in a disparaging tone, the contents of Schenck's leaflet. "In impassioned language it intimated that conscription was despotism in its worst form and a monstrous wrong against humanity in the interest of Wall Street's chosen few."

How does the leaflet violate the law? Drawing on the "bad tendency" test that courts traditionally had used to evaluate controversial speech, Holmes suggested it was a matter of common sense to conclude that the leaflet was aimed at discouraging conscription. "The document would not have been sent unless it had been intended to have some effect, and we do not see what effect it could be expected to have upon persons subject to the draft except to influence them to obstruct the carrying of it out," Holmes wrote.

Furthermore, Holmes said, showing that the leaflet actually succeeded in encouraging defiance of the draft was not necessary. "If the act (speaking or circulating a paper), its tendency and the intent with which it is done are the same, we perceive no ground for saying that success alone warrants making the act a crime."

Any qualms about restricting speech that ought to be protected by the First Amendment, Holmes concluded, should be alleviated by realizing that in times of war, extraordinary restrictions may be necessary.

EXCERPTS

From Justice Holmes's majority opinion: "We admit that in many places and in ordinary times the defendants in saying all that was said in the circular would have been within their constitutional rights. But the character of every act depends upon the circumstances in which it is done. The most stringent protection of free speech would not protect a man in falsely shouting fire in a theatre and causing a panic. It does not even protect a man from an injunction against uttering words that may have all the effect of force. The question in every case is whether the words used are used in such circumstances and are of such a nature as to create a clear and present danger that they will bring about the substantive evils that Congress has a right to prevent. It is a question of proximity and degree. When a nation is at war many things that might be said in time of peace are such a hindrance to its effort that their utterance will not be endured so long as men fight and that no court could regard them as protected by any constitutional right."

IMPACT

Justice Holmes's brief ruling in *Schenck* includes some of the most familiar phrases contained in a Supreme Court opinion. "Clear and present danger" and "falsely shouting fire in a theatre" have become shorthand ways of expressing the limits to the protection of speech provided by the First Amendment.

But since Holmes used the phrase "clear and present danger," he and other judges have interpreted it in a variety of ways — some more protective of speech than others. Chief Justice William Rehnquist, writing in *All the Laws But One*, a 1998 book on civil liberties in wartime, said of *Schenck*, "This notable opinion put some flesh and bones on the First Amendment, but Holmes's formula, like most formulas, raised questions of its own."

In *Schenck*, Holmes seemed to be saying that speech could be restricted if it had the tendency to cause a violation of law. In decisions a week after *Schenck*, one upholding the conviction of Socialist Party leader and presidential candidate Eugene V. Debs, Holmes repeated that view.

By November of that year, however, Holmes changed his views — perhaps persuaded by Hand's arguments. In *Abrams v. United States*, the Court upheld another Sedition Act prosecution, citing *Schenck*. This time Holmes dissented, arguing that to justify restriction of speech, the danger to the country had to be not only "clear and present" but also immediate. Suppressing speech when the threat is not imminent would do damage to the "marketplace of ideas" essential to a democracy, he said.

Since *Abrams*, the test has shifted even further to allow all speech except that which can be proven to incite direct and immediate violations of the law. Schenck was the Court's starting point on a path that has led to an extraordinary level of protection for even the most unpopular and hateful speech. "The modern First Amendment began" the day Schenck was handed down, said First Amendment scholar Ronald Collins.

In the 1969 ruling *Brandenburg v. Ohio*, the Court in effect abandoned — though did not explicitly overrule — the "clear and present danger" test, instead calling for proof of the likelihood of "imminent lawless action" before a speaker can be punished.

One further note: *Schenck* is often described as the first case in which the Supreme Court was asked to overturn a federal law on the basis of First Amendment free speech grounds. In the 1997 book *Free Speech in Its Forgotten Years*, University of Texas law professor David Rabban suggests that is not the case. He describes numerous free speech debates and lawsuits that resulted in First Amendment rulings by the Supreme Court and the lower courts in the late nineteenth and early twentieth century.

KOREMATSU v. UNITED STATES

Subject:	War powers
Decided:	December 18, 1944
Chief Justice:	Harlan Fiske Stone (D, Franklin Roosevelt appointee)
Petitioner:	Fred Korematsu, relocated Japanese American citizen
Respondent:	United States government
Vote:	6-3 for United States government
Majority Opinion:	Justice Hugo L. Black
	323 U.S. 214
	laws.findlaw.com/US/323/214.html

DECISION

All laws that limit the rights of people because of their race are automatically suspect and can be justified only very rarely, such as in wartime. However, it was within the war powers of Congress and the president to remove Japanese Americans from areas on the West Coast near military installations in wartime.

BACKGROUND

Following the attack by Japan on the U.S. fleet at Pearl Harbor, Hawaii, on December 7, 1941, a wave of anti-Japanese animosity and panic swept the United States, particularly on the West Coast. Rumors that Japan was planning to attack West Coast military installations, aided by espionage and sabotage by Japanese Americans, fueled the panic.

Fred Korematsu, relocated Japanese American citizen.
Photo courtesy of Karen Korematsu and the Fred T. Korematsu Institute

"The Japanese in California should be under armed guard to the last man and woman right now — and to hell with *habeas corpus* until the danger is over," wrote popular conservative columnist Westbrook Pegler soon after Pearl Harbor. Among those supporting relocation of Japanese Americans was California governor Earl Warren, who would later become chief justice of the United States.

President Franklin Roosevelt in February 1942 issued an order authorizing the War Department to exclude anyone — regardless of ethnic heritage — from designated zones around military facilities on the West Coast. His aides later indicated that Roosevelt was not deterred by any constitutional issues. "The Constitution has not greatly bothered any wartime president," wrote Attorney General Francis Biddle, who opposed the order.

Military officials responded first by imposing a curfew on people of Japanese ancestry and then by ordering the "exclusion" of this group altogether. Within months, more than 120,000 people of Japanese descent, 70,000 of them U.S. citizens, were moved to ten relocation centers away from the coast. The fact that many of these detainees had deep ties to the United States and showed not the slightest evidence of sympathy with Japan in the war effort did not prevent their removal.

Gen. John DeWitt, justifying the exclusion order before a congressional panel, said, "A Jap's a Jap. It makes no difference whether he is an American citizen or not. I have no confidence in their loyalty whatsoever."

One of those relocated was Fred Korematsu, a Japanese American born in Oakland, California. Korematsu had tried to enlist in the U.S. Army before Pearl Harbor, but was rejected for medical reasons. When the order to evacuate Japanese Americans was issued, he tried to avoid capture by changing his name and having some minor plastic surgery that he hoped would make him appear Hispanic. But he was arrested in San Leandro, California, in May 1942 for remaining in a military zone in violation of the evacuation order. After a jailhouse visit from a lawyer from the American Civil Liberties Union, Korematsu agreed to make a test case to challenge the constitutionality of the evacuation.

While his case was making its way to the Supreme Court, the justices issued a decision upholding the curfew imposed on Japanese Americans. In the May 1943 ruling in *Hirabayashi v. United States*, the Court said the constitutional war power included the "power to wage war successfully," justifying measures such as a curfew. But the Court specifically limited its ruling to the curfew order, avoiding the evacuation issue. Some scholars believe the Court was hoping that the evacuation program would soon be ended, making the constitutional issue moot.

But the program was still in place when the Court considered Korematsu's case in 1944. The U.S. government offered a new justification for the internment program: it protected Japanese Americans from racial hostility they might encounter if they were allowed to return to their homes.

VOTE

6-3, with Justice Hugo L. Black writing for the majority. Joining him were Chief Justice Harlan Fiske Stone and Justices Stanley F. Reed, Felix Frankfurter, William O. Douglas, and Wiley B. Rutledge. Dissenting were Justices Owen J. Roberts, Frank W. Murphy, and Robert H. Jackson.

HIGHLIGHTS

The decision began, ironically, with a ringing condemnation of laws that treat people differently because of racial animosity. "It should be noted, to begin with, that all legal restrictions which curtail the civil rights of a single racial group are immediately suspect. That is not to say that all such restrictions are unconstitutional. It is to say that courts must subject them to the most rigid scrutiny. Pressing public necessity may sometimes justify the existence of such restrictions; racial antagonism never can."

But the evacuation order and the federal law that backed it up, the Court concluded, were not the product of racial antagonism. Deferring completely to the judgment of military officials, the Court said the evacuation could be justified. "The judgment that exclusion of the whole group was ... a military imperative answers the contention that the exclusion was in the nature of group punishment based on antagonism to those of Japanese origin." The Court noted that some Japanese Americans had refused to pledge allegiance to the United States, and that some detainees had sought to move to Japan.

The Court also went out of its way to limit the scope of the decision. Although critics of the evacuation order said it could not be distinguished from the accompanying placement of evacuees in relocation centers, the Court said it was ruling only on the former. "Regardless of the true nature of the assembly and relocation centers — and we deem it unjustifiable to call them concentration camps, with all the ugly connotations that term implies — we are dealing specifically with nothing but an exclusion order." The Court said, "it will be time enough to decide" the constitutionality of the detention centers in a separate case.

Justice Frankfurter wrote a concurring opinion that was also deferential toward the military but hinted that he did not necessarily approve of the evacuation of Japanese Americans. "To find that the Constitution does not forbid the military measures now complained of does not carry with it approval of that which Congress and the Executive did. That is their business, not ours."

The three dissenting justices wrote separately to underline their distaste for the Court's decision. Justice Roberts said that Korematsu had been convicted "as a punishment for not submitting to imprisonment in a concentration camp, based on his ancestry, and solely because of his ancestry, without evidence or inquiry concerning his loyalty and good disposition towards the United States. If this be a correct statement of the facts disclosed by this record, and facts of which we take judicial notice, I need hardly labor the conclusion that Constitutional rights have been violated."

To Justice Murphy, the exclusion order went "over 'the very brink of constitutional power' and ... into the ugly abyss of racism.... . Racial discrimination in any form and in any degree has no justifiable part whatever in our democratic way of life. It is unattractive in any setting, but it is utterly revolting among a free people who have embraced the principles set forth in the Constitution of the United States."

Justice Jackson bluntly minimized the "crime" for which Korematsu had been imprisoned. "Korematsu ... has been convicted of an act not commonly a crime. It consists merely of being present in the state whereof he is a citizen, near the place where he was born, and where all his life he has lived."

In another memorable passage, Jackson said, "The Court for all time has validated the principle of racial discrimination in criminal procedure and of transplanting American citizens. The principle then lies about like a loaded weapon, ready for the hand of any authority that can bring forward a plausible claim of an urgent need."

EXCERPTS

From Justice Black's majority opinion: "[W]e are unable to conclude that it was beyond the war power of Congress and the Executive to exclude those of Japanese ancestry from the West Coast war area at the time they did. True, exclusion from the area in which one's home is located is a far greater deprivation than constant confinement to the home from 8 p.m. to 6 a.m. Nothing short of apprehension by the proper military authorities of the gravest imminent danger to the public safety can constitutionally justify either. But exclusion from a threatened area, no less than curfew, has a definite and close relationship to the prevention of espionage and sabotage. The military authorities, charged with the primary responsibility of defending our shores, concluded that curfew provided inadequate protection and ordered exclusion... .

"... Citizenship has its responsibilities as well as its privileges, and in time of war the burden is always heavier. Compulsory exclusion of large groups of citizens from their homes, except under circumstances of direst emergency and peril, is inconsistent with our basic governmental institutions. But when under conditions of modern warfare our shores are threatened by hostile forces, the power to protect must be commensurate with the threatened danger.

". . . Korematsu was not excluded from the Military Area because of hostility to him or his race. He was excluded because we are at war with the Japanese Empire, because the properly constituted military authorities feared an invasion of our West Coast and felt constrained to take proper security measures, because they decided that the military urgency of the situation demanded that all citizens of Japanese ancestry be segregated from the West Coast temporarily, and finally, because Congress, reposing its confidence in this time of war in our military leaders — as inevitably it must — determined that they should have the power to do just this."

IMPACT

Korematsu is often ranked, along with *Scott v. Sandford* and *Plessy v. Ferguson*, as one of the Court's worst and most embarrassing decisions. More than seven decades later, it seems inconceivable to many that the Supreme Court would have approved the wholesale evacuation of U.S. citizens chosen solely because of their race and heritage.

Justice Black, who was otherwise known as a defender of civil liberties, was troubled by his authorship of *Korematsu* for the rest of his life, according to biographer Roger Newman. But Black persisted in defending it as a correct decision, given the necessities of war. In 1967 he told an interviewer, "Had they [the Japanese] attacked our shores you'd have had a large number [of Japanese Americans] fighting with the Japanese troops. And a lot of innocent Japanese Americans would have been shot in the panic. Under these circumstances I saw nothing wrong in moving them away from the danger area."

The impact of the decision on the evacuation program was limited. By the time Korematsu was handed down, the threat of Japanese invasion, if there ever was one, had dissipated. On the same day *Korematsu* was issued, the Court decided a separate *habeas corpus* case, *Ex parte Endo*, in a seemingly contradictory way. Although it did not pass judgment on the entire relocation program, the *Endo* ruling said that Japanese Americans could not be detained if there was no evidence of their disloyalty to the nation. Perhaps aware that the decision was coming down, the War Department announced a day before the Court acted that detainees "whose records have stood the test of Army scrutiny" would be allowed to return home. The detention centers closed, and Japanese Americans rebuilt their lives and businesses with no further interference.

But the internment had a lasting impact on detainees. In the 1970s Japanese American organizations began pressing Congress for compensation for their wartime deprivations. Congress in 1980 created a commission to look into the issue. It heard testimony from hundreds of detainees and recommended that each survivor of the camps be given $20,000 as compensation. The compensation was approved, but by the time the checks were distributed, many of the detainees had died. Under President Ronald Reagan, the nation formally apologized for the internment of Japanese Americans.

At the same time, a legal campaign was launched to overturn Korematsu's conviction. As part of the campaign, political science professor Peter Irons, author of several books on the Supreme Court, obtained the Justice Department's files on the case and several others through the Freedom of Information Act. In the files Irons said he found "smoking guns of legal misconduct," showing that the government had no proof of disloyalty by Japanese Americans before it ordered the evacuation. The government misled the justices in the *Korematsu* case, Irons asserts.

Fred Korematsu's conviction was overturned in 1983. Completing the long saga, President Bill Clinton in 1998 presented Korematsu with the Presidential Medal of Freedom. "Fred Korematsu deserves our respect and thanks for his patient pursuit to preserve the civil liberties we hold dear," Clinton said.

Korematsu continued his activism until his death in 2005 at age 86. He filed friend-of-the-court briefs in post-9/11 Supreme Court cases involving detainees at Guantanamo Bay Detention Camp, as well as for Jose Padilla, an American citizen detained in the United States as an enemy combatant. His brief in the Padilla case stated, "By allowing the Executive Branch to decide unilaterally who to detain, and for how long, our country will repeat the same mistakes of the past."

YOUNGSTOWN SHEET & TUBE CO. v. SAWYER

Subject:	Separation of powers
Decided:	June 2, 1952
Chief Justice:	Fred M. Vinson (D, Truman appointee)
Petitioner:	Youngstown Sheet & Tube Company, a steel mill
Respondent:	Charles Sawyer, U.S. secretary of commerce
Vote:	6-3 for Youngstown Sheet & Tube Company
Majority Opinion:	Justice Hugo L. Black
	343 U.S. 579
	laws.findlaw.com/US/343/579.html

DECISION

President Truman did not have the power under the Constitution or any law to order the seizure of the nation's steel mills to prevent a labor strike. Only Congress, through legislation, could authorize such a seizure.

BACKGROUND

Congress never declared war in the Korean "conflict," but it was a war nevertheless. Repelling the invasion of South Korea by troops from the north, which began in June 1950, was a massive undertaking for the United States, costing more than 33,000 U.S. lives and billions of dollars in arms and equipment.

The U.S. economy was on a war footing to produce what was needed for the U.S. troops. So when a labor dispute between the United Steelworkers of America and the steel industry threatened to trigger a strike that would shut down the nation's steel mills, President Harry S. Truman felt the need to act quickly.

On April 4, 1952, the union signaled that a strike was imminent. Five days later, after mediation efforts failed, Truman issued an executive order directing a cabinet member, Secretary of Commerce Charles Sawyer, to seize and operate the mills. Truman noted that "steel is an indispensable component of substantially all ... weapons and materials" needed in the war, making the action essential to the national interest. As soon as the order was issued, the union called off the strike. U.S. flags were hoisted over the steel mills, and production continued as usual.

It was an extraordinary but not unprecedented action. In previous wars, presidents had seized businesses and private facilities deemed necessary for national security, but most of those seizures had been authorized by federal law. The steel companies affected by the current order, led by the Youngstown firm, went to court claiming that Truman was acting without any congressional or constitutional authorization.

Truman believed his authority to act was based, among other things, on the president's constitutional role as commander in chief. In addition, Truman may have been emboldened by the fact that four of the justices were his own appointees, and some of the others shared an expansive, Roosevelt-era view of the powers of the presidency. Historians have reported that Truman met privately with Chief Justice Fred M. Vinson before issuing the order and received assurances that the seizure was constitutional.

Because of the urgency of the issue, the courts expedited the case. A trial judge ruled against the Truman administration, and an appeals court propelled the case directly to the Supreme Court. On May 12, just over a month after the seizure order was issued, the justices heard oral arguments. As soon as the justices met in conference, it was clear that Vinson's calculations had been wrong.

VOTE

6-3, with Justice Hugo L. Black writing the majority opinion. Joining him were Justices Felix Frankfurter, William O. Douglas, Robert H.

Jackson, Harold H. Burton, and Tom C. Clark. Dissenting were Chief Justice Fred M. Vinson and Justices Stanley F. Reed and Sherman Minton.

HIGHLIGHTS

The majority and the dissenters took nearly opposite views of presidential powers and constitutional interpretation. Justice Black took a literal approach, asserting that if neither the Constitution nor any act of Congress authorized the president's action, it could not be permitted. "The President's power, if any, to issue the order must stem either from an act of Congress or from the Constitution itself," Black declared.

As Melvin Urofsky put it in his book *Division and Discord*, Chief Justice Vinson's view was quite the opposite: "The president could, in response to a national emergency, do everything except what had been specifically prohibited."

Black argued that, if anything, Congress had considered and rejected the notion of allowing presidents to seize property as a way of ending labor disputes. When Congress debated passage of the Taft-Hartley Act in 1947, legislators had decided that allowing seizures would interfere with collective bargaining. Instead, the law authorized other ways of preventing harmful strikes, including a "cooling-off" period, an avenue that Truman had not tried in the steel dispute.

No other law authorized the seizure, Black wrote, nor did any provision of the Constitution or the president's general powers as commander in chief. Only Congress, Black concluded, had the power to do what Truman had tried to do. "The power of Congress to adopt such public policies as those proclaimed by the order is beyond question," wrote Black. "It can authorize the taking of private property for public use. It can make laws regulating the relationships between employers and employees, prescribing rules designed to settle labor disputes, and fixing wages and working conditions in certain fields of our economy. The Constitution does not subject this law-making power of Congress to presidential or military supervision or control."

Justice Frankfurter, in a concurring opinion, reviewed the history of other presidential seizures in time of war, and found that most had been authorized by Congress. "A scheme of government like ours no doubt at times feels the lack of power to act with complete, all-embracing, swiftly moving authority," Frankfurter wrote. "No doubt a government with distributed authority, subject to be challenged in the courts of law, at least long enough to consider and adjudicate the challenge, labors under restrictions from which other governments are free. It has not been our tradition to envy such governments. In any event our government was designed to have such restrictions."

Justice Douglas agreed. "We pay a price for our system of checks and balances, for the distribution of power among the three branches of government. It is a price that today may seem exorbitant to many. Today a kindly President uses the seizure power to effect a wage increase and to keep the steel furnaces in production. Yet tomorrow, another President might use the same power to prevent a wage increase, to curb trade-unionists, to regiment labor as oppressively as industry thinks it has been regimented by this seizure."

In another concurrence, Justice Jackson wrote, "When the President takes measures incompatible with the expressed or implied will of Congress, his power is at its lowest ebb.... Presidential claim to a power at once so conclusive and preclusive must be scrutinized with caution, for what is at stake is the equilibrium established by our constitutional system."

Chief Justice Vinson's dissent argued that the president's power should be at its height in times of crisis. Under the majority's view, Vinson wrote, "the President is left powerless at the very moment when the need for action may be most pressing and when no one, other than he, is immediately capable of action. Under this view, he is left powerless because a power not expressly given to Congress is nevertheless found to rest exclusively with Congress."

The Framers of the Constitution, Vinson said, could not have intended to hamstring a president in time of war. "History bears out the genius of the Founding Fathers, who created a Government subject to law but not left subject to inertia when vigor and initiative are required."

EXCERPTS

From Justice Black's majority opinion: "There is no statute that expressly authorizes the President to take possession of property as he did here. Nor is there any act of Congress to which our attention has been directed from which such a power can fairly be implied... .

"The order cannot properly be sustained as an exercise of the President's military power as Commander in Chief of the Armed Forces. The Government attempts to do so by citing a number of cases upholding broad powers in military commanders engaged in day-to-day fighting in a theater of war. Such cases need not concern us here. Even though 'theater of war' be an expanding concept, we cannot with faithfulness to our constitutional system hold that the Commander in Chief of the Armed Forces has the ultimate power as such to take possession of private property in order to keep labor disputes from stopping production. This is a job for the Nation's lawmakers, not for its military authorities.... .

"The Founders of this Nation entrusted the lawmaking power to the Congress alone in both good and bad times. It would do no good to recall the historical events, the fears of power and the hopes for freedom that lay behind their choice. Such a review would but confirm our holding that this seizure order cannot stand."

IMPACT

The so-called "steel seizure" case, and the reaction to it, serves as a case study of the role of the Supreme Court in the national government. Even in time of war and under pressure from the president, the Supreme Court did not hesitate to tell the president he was flat-out wrong. No matter how important the short-term need, the Court said the constitutional framework had to be followed. *The Economist* in London wrote, "The Supreme Court ... has once more brought to heel the mighty: the President, the union, the industry, and Congress."

President Truman, although unhappy with the decision, did not hesitate to obey it. He returned the steel mills to their owners. The steelworkers went on strike, and the strike was soon settled, with wage increases for the workers and price increases for the producers.

Truman biographer David McCullough wrote that after the decision came down, Justice Black invited the president and other justices to a party at his home in Alexandria, Virginia. At first Truman seemed cool, but after some drinks and food, Truman turned to Black and said, "Hugo, I don't much care for your law, but, by golly, this bourbon is good."

The Court's ruling is often cited not just as a check on presidential power but as a celebration of the checks and balances the Constitution envisioned for the three branches of government. Justice Jackson's formulation in his concurring opinion in *Youngstown Sheet & Tube* is often quoted to make the point that a separate, interdependent, and flexible system works best. "While the Constitution diffuses power the better to secure liberty, it also contemplates that practice will integrate the dispersed powers into a workable government. It enjoins upon its branches separateness but interdependence, autonomy but reciprocity. Presidential powers are not fixed but fluctuate, depending upon their disjunction or conjunction with those of Congress."

That principle returned to the fore in landmark cases decided by the Court stemming from the "war on terror." In *Hamdi v. Rumsfeld*, when Justice Sandra Day O'Connor wrote for the Court that a state of war does not give presidents a "blank check" to violate constitutional principles, she cited *Youngstown* as her main support. In 2006, *Youngstown* was also cited in *Hamdan v. Rumsfeld*, which found that a system of military commissions established to try Guantanamo detainees had not been authorized by Congress.

In June 2015, *Youngstown* also provided the framework for the Court's decision in *Zivotofsky v. Kerry*, which said the president has exclusive power to give diplomatic recognition to foreign sovereigns.

President Harry S. Truman. Source: Library of Congress

BROWN v. BOARD OF EDUCATION OF TOPEKA

Subject:	School desegregation
Decided:	May 17, 1954
Chief Justice:	Fred M. Vinson (D, Truman appointee)
Petitioner:	Oliver Brown, on behalf of his daughter, Linda, an African American student
Respondent:	The Board of Education of Topeka
Vote:	9-0 for Brown
Majority Opinion:	Chief Justice Earl Warren
	347 U.S. 483
	laws.findlaw.com/US/347/483.html

DECISION

Separate public schools for blacks and whites are inherently unequal. States that maintain racially segregated schools violate the Fourteenth Amendment's guarantee of equal protection of the laws.

BACKGROUND

The North's victory in the Civil War and the constitutional amendments that followed the war did not guarantee equality for blacks in the United States. In ruling on a Louisiana law that required separate facilities for blacks and whites on trains, the Supreme Court upheld in *Plessy v. Ferguson* the constitutionality of "separate but equal" accommodations. The 1896 decision gave the Court's blessing to a wide range of segregated services. So-called Jim Crow laws embedded segregation deep into the U.S. fabric. Seventeen states and the District of Columbia had laws requiring segregated schools.

Plaintiffs in Brown v. Board of Education
of Topeka *including Linda Brown (front
row, third from left) and her father Oliver
Brown (back row, second from left).*
Photo by Carl Iwasaki/The LIFE Picture
Collection/Getty Images

Segregation in public schools had condemned generations of black children to lower-quality education because their schools were uniformly neglected, underequipped, and understaffed. But soon after World War II, as black soldiers who had fought hard for their country returned to the United States, demands for an end to segregation, especially in the schools, began to be heard.

Thurgood Marshall, then a young civil rights lawyer and later the Supreme Court's first black justice, believed that the time had come to mount a legal assault on *Plessy* and on school segregation. Faint signs of hope were beginning to emerge in some Supreme Court rulings. In a 1948 case *Shelley v. Kraemer*, the Court ruled that states could not enforce racial restrictions on property ownership. Two years later, in *Sweatt v. Painter*, the Court told the state of Texas that its law school established for blacks could not be viewed as equal in any way to the all-white University of Texas Law School. The *Sweatt* ruling did not overturn *Plessy*, but it did suggest that public educational institutions for blacks had to be truly equal to those for whites for their separateness to be constitutional.

The challenge for Marshall was to show that separate schools could never be equal. He was not at all confident that the Supreme Court would rule that way, but he and the National Association for the Advancement of Colored People (NAACP) decided the effort should be made. "Thurgood Marshall came down for boldness," wrote Richard Kluger in *Simple Justice*, the classic book about the *Brown* case.

In several states and the District of Columbia, courageous African American families began to file highly unpopular lawsuits to challenge school segregation. In the end, five separate cases went before the Supreme Court, and the decision became known by the name of one of them, *Brown v. Board of Education*.

Oliver Brown sued the school board in Topeka, Kansas, on behalf of his daughter Linda to challenge that city's segregated system. Linda Brown had to walk between railroad tracks to catch a bus to the all-black Monroe School, even though she lived just a few blocks from the all-white Sumner School. "Sometimes I was just so cold that I cried all the way to the bus stop," she later recalled. In the fall of 1950 Oliver Brown tried to enroll seven-year-old Linda in the third grade at Sumner. When he was turned away, Brown went to the NAACP, which filed suit.

The second case, *Briggs v. Elliott*, was from South Carolina. Harry Briggs Jr. and more than sixty other black parents sued the Clarendon

County schools to demand equal school facilities. White children there rode buses to modern schools; black children had to walk as far as five miles to get to separate, ramshackle schools. In *Davis v. County School Board of Prince Edward County, Virginia*, high school students challenged Virginia's segregated schools. Students at all-black Moton High School in Farmville had staged a highly unusual strike to protest the poor facilities at the school, and 117 of them, led by ninth-grader Dorothy Davis, filed suit. *Gebhart v. Belton* was a Delaware case brought by Ethel Belton and seven other black Claymont parents whose children had to travel to downtown Wilmington to attend an all-black high school that was inferior to the white school. The final case, *Bolling v. Sharpe*, was filed on behalf of twelve-year-old Spotswood Bolling Jr. to challenge segregated schools in Washington, D.C. It was ultimately ruled on separately from the others, because of the District of Columbia's status as a federal city not governed by state laws.

In the lower courts the black plaintiffs seeking school equality had lost in all but the Delaware case, where schools were ordered desegregated in 1952.

In spite of recent rulings that supported the rights of minorities, the Supreme Court was not eager to take on the issue of public school segregation or to consider overturning *Plessy* outright. Chief Justice Fred M. Vinson, in particular, was reluctant to overturn the settled tradition of separate schools. Hugo L. Black and William O. Douglas were the only two justices eager to overrule *Plessy*.

Lawyers argued the cases over three days in December 1952. Thurgood Marshall made a forceful argument that segregated schools were the result of "an inherent determination that the people who were formerly in slavery ... shall be kept as near that stage as is possible." In legal briefs, Marshall had cited the work of psychologist Kenneth Clark, who in the 1940s devised a simple test to assess the self-image of young black children. Clark showed the children four dolls — two white and two brown — and asked them to choose the doll they thought looked "nice" or liked the best. Among black children from Massachusetts to Arkansas, a significant majority showed "an unmistakable preference" for the white dolls. To Clark, this experiment proved that black children had low self-esteem.

Virginia's attorney general, J. Lindsay Almond Jr., told the justices that an order from the Supreme Court to desegregate schools "would destroy the public school system in Virginia." Almond, like many in the South, thought that local officials would shut down public schools altogether rather than integrate them.

Arguing in the Briggs case on behalf of South Carolina's segregated schools was John W. Davis, a former presidential candidate who was perhaps the best known and most accomplished advocate before the Supreme Court of that time. He voiced doubt about whether black families really wanted integration in their schools or even would be better off in integrated schools. He mocked the use of social science evidence — including Clark's doll experiment — by civil rights groups favoring desegregation. "Much of that which is handed around under the name of social science is an effort on the part of the scientist to rationalize his own preconceptions."

Based on the questioning from the justices, Marshall emerged from the arguments worried about whether a majority of the Court was prepared to order school desegregation. As months went by, his concern increased. In May 1953 the Court ordered the case to be reargued in the fall. Justice Frankfurter had urged this course of action after seeing how divided the justices were. The Court also asked the U.S. attorney general to participate in the second set of arguments — a request that forced the new Eisenhower administration to decide where it stood. After some early reluctance, President Dwight Eisenhower agreed that his administration would join the case on the side of desegregation.

Before the cases could be reargued, an unexpected development completely changed the outlook: a new chief justice took over at the Court. In September 1953 Chief Justice Vinson suffered a heart attack and died. Eisenhower named Gov. Earl Warren of California to replace Vinson.

What probably would have been a 5-4 majority in favor of overturning *Plessy* turned into a unanimous 9-0 vote. Warren was determined that the Court should present a united front to the nation, and he had the skill to persuade the other justices that it was important to do so. In his memoir however, Warren insisted "there was no dissension within the Court" on the outcome of the *Brown* cases. "There was not even vigorous argument." Warren wrote the decision himself, deliberately keeping it short and devoid of legal jargon so that it could be widely read and understood. To emphasize the Court's unanimity, on the day when the decision was announced Justice Robert Jackson, who had suffered a heart attack, left his sickbed to be on the bench.

VOTE

9-0, with Chief Justice Earl Warren writing the opinion for the Court. Joining him were Justices Hugo L. Black, Stanley F. Reed, Felix Frank-furter, William O. Douglas, Robert H. Jackson, Harold H. Burton, Tom C. Clark, and Sherman Minton.

HIGHLIGHTS

The Court's decision to overturn *Plessy*, after nearly sixty years of living with its "separate but equal" doctrine, could not occur without at least a glance toward history. When the Fourteenth Amendment was ratified in 1868 with its guarantee of equal protection of the laws, did the drafters have public education in mind?

Chief Justice Warren determined, however, that history was of little help on that point. Public education was in its infancy then, and in many states did not exist; where it did exist, blacks were barred outright from benefiting from it. "In approaching this problem, we cannot turn the clock back to 1868, when the Amendment was adopted, or even to 1896, when *Plessy v. Ferguson* was written," Warren wrote. "We must consider public education in the light of its full development and its present place in American life throughout the Nation."

Now, the Court agreed, public education is one of the most important services that government provides. Its importance transformed public education into a right that should be made available to all equally, in the Court's view.

The crucial next question was whether providing separate schools for blacks and whites is, in itself, a violation of that right to equal education. The Court ruled that unquestionably it did. Separate school facilities for blacks and whites have no place in U.S. society anymore, the Court said. To bolster the point, the Court took the unusual step of citing psychological evidence — notably Kenneth Clark's research, and Gunnar Myrdal's book *An American Dilemma* — to conclude that segregation has a detrimental effect on black children. "Whatever may have been the extent of psychological knowledge at the time of *Plessy v. Ferguson*, this finding is amply supported by modern authority," Warren wrote.

Partly to keep the opinion uncluttered and partly to win over Justice Reed, Warren in the opinion's last paragraph put off any detailed decree or order telling states and school boards what they must do to comply with the Court's ruling. Citing the "considerable complexity" of the task of remedying segregation, the Court scheduled arguments for the fall on the question of "appropriate relief." By avoiding several controversial issues, Warren was able to fashion a unanimous decision that spoke with force, if not specificity.

In the separate opinion *Bolling v. Sharpe*, handed down the same day, the unanimous Court said segregation was equally unacceptable in District of Columbia schools. "In view of our decision that the Constitution prohibits the states from maintaining racially segregated public schools, it would be unthinkable that the same Constitution would impose a lesser duty on the Federal Government," Warren wrote for the Court.

EXCERPTS

From Chief Justice Warren's majority opinion: "Compulsory school attendance laws and the great expenditures for education both demonstrate our recognition of the importance of education to our democratic society. It is required in the performance of our most basic public responsibilities, even service in the armed forces. It is the very foundation of good citizenship. Today it is a principal instrument in awakening the child to cultural values, in preparing him for later professional training, and in helping him to adjust normally to his environment. In these days, it is doubtful that any child may reasonably be expected to succeed in life if he is denied the opportunity of an education. Such an opportunity, where the state has undertaken to provide it, is a right which must be made available to all on equal terms.

"We come then to the question presented: Does segregation of children in public schools solely on the basis of race, even though the physical facilities and other 'tangible' factors may be equal, deprive the children of the minority group of equal educational opportunities? We believe that it does... .

"We conclude that in the field of public education the doctrine of 'separate but equal' has no place. Separate educational facilities are inherently unequal. Therefore, we hold that the plaintiffs and others similarly situated for whom the actions have been brought are, by reason of the segregation complained of, deprived of the equal protection of the laws guaranteed by the Fourteenth Amendment."

IMPACT

With its power and simplicity, the *Brown* decision stands as one of the most important and best known the Court has ever issued. In a single stroke, the Court swept aside centuries of custom, replacing it with a command to work toward the democratic ideal of equality. Where the other branches of government showed ambivalence over issues of race, the Supreme Court spoke firmly.

"This is a day that will live in glory," Justice Frankfurter said in a handwritten note to Warren the day *Brown* was handed down. Thurgood Marshall, who had apparently been tipped off that the decision was coming, was in the Court that day and later recalled, "I was so happy I was numb." By later that day, the euphoria wore off and Marshall realized that "the fight has just begun."

Marshall was correct. Even though the Court had deftly put off the issue of how quickly desegregation should be achieved, it had to deal with that issue again, and it had to face a South that was determined not to change. Many officials in the South labeled the day of the decision "Black Monday." Sen. Harry Byrd of Virginia pledged "massive resistance." Most southern members of Congress signed a "southern manifesto" denouncing the decision.

When the Court reconvened to hear arguments on how to implement *Brown*, it became clear how massive and difficult this endeavor would be. S. Emory Rogers, arguing for segregated schools in South Carolina, said to the Court candidly, "I would have to tell you that right now we would not conform — we would not send our white children to the Negro schools."

On May 31, 1955, the Court handed down what would become known as *Brown II*. Again, the Court spoke with brevity, ordering that the nation's schools desegregate with "all deliberate speed." No specific date was fixed, and many southern states took that as permission to make no progress at all. Some states moved to repeal compulsory attendance laws and to help set up private "academies" that would be able to remain all-white. In many communities, black parents who led efforts to integrate local schools were fired from their jobs and threatened with violence.

In 1957 Gov. Orval Faubus of Arkansas ordered members of the National Guard to physically prevent black students from attending Little Rock's Central High School, defying a post-*Brown* order from a federal judge. Faubus responded to a court order by withdrawing the guard and permitting violence to break out. Reluctantly, President Eisenhower federalized the National Guard and ordered U.S. Army troops to Little Rock to restore order and escort black students to their classes.

Following the turmoil in Little Rock, a federal judge gave permission to the school board to delay full desegregation for two and a half years. The NAACP challenged the delay in court, filing a lawsuit that eventually made its way to the Supreme Court. In the 1958 ruling *Cooper v. Aaron*, all nine justices joined an opinion expressing their anger at the resistance to *Brown* that was being displayed by local officials. "No state legislator or executive or judicial officer can war against the Constitution without violating his undertaking to support it," the Court said.

Other decisions also reaffirmed *Brown*, but resistance continued. Shifts in housing patterns that left many urban neighborhoods dominated by one race or another also kept schools segregated. "Despite all the bends in the road, school desegregation has not retreated," wrote Kluger in *Simple Justice*. Over the years, meanwhile, some blacks changed their views about desegregation. They argued that the concept underlying *Brown* was insulting to blacks, because it seemed to suggest that any school setting without whites was automatically inferior. Many black families also objected to the long bus rides for their children that were part of many desegregation plans.

In the middle 1990s, encouraged by several rulings from a more conservative Supreme Court, federal judges closed the book on many school district desegregation plans, declaring that local officials had made a good-faith effort to end segregation. Partly because of these developments, decreasing numbers of black students are attending integrated schools. According to Gary Orfield, director of the Harvard Project on School Desegregation, even when minority families move to mostly white suburbs, they often end up attending mostly nonwhite schools. "Progress toward desegregation in U.S. public schools is being steadily reversed," the Harvard project reported.

Some commentators concluded that in fact little progress had been made toward equality in education for blacks. "Many public schools are as racially isolated and unequal today as when the Supreme Court spoke 45 years ago," *Washington Post* columnist Colbert I. King wrote in 1999. The NAACP Legal Defense and Educational Fund concluded that "over the last 50 years, the segregation of African Americans has actually increased or changed very little."

In a 1999 speech marking the forty-fifth anniversary of *Brown*, Secretary of Housing and Urban Development Andrew Cuomo offered an assessment that, in most respects, could have been given before *Brown* was handed down. "The truth is, we are moving to two education systems…. You can go into one school in a suburban district, and they have all the tools and all the equipment. They take the first-graders, they bring them in and they put them on the Internet. The other side of town, the urban school district, they don't have a basketball net."

On the occasion of the 60th anniversary of the decision in 2014, Sherrilyn Ifill, president and director-counsel of the NAACP Legal Defense and Education Fund said, "*Brown* was no magic bullet for the problems of race and inequality that have plagued our nation since its beginning. We proudly celebrate *Brown* even as we recognize the ongoing, difficult challenges we face today not only in education, but in criminal justice, in economic opportunity and at the ballot box…. At its core, civil rights work is the work of democracy maintenance."

President Barack Obama, the nation's first African American president, also marked the anniversary with words of celebration and concern. "*Brown v. Board of Education* shifted the legal and moral compass of our nation," he said in a proclamation. "Yet the Supreme Court alone could not destroy segregation … The hope and promise of *Brown* remains unfulfilled."

MAPP v. OHIO

Subject:	Search and seizure
Decided:	June 19, 1961
Chief Justice:	Earl Warren (R, Eisenhower appointee)
Petitioner:	Dollree Mapp, Ohioan appealing conviction for pornography posession
Respondent:	State of Ohio
Vote:	5-4 for Mapp
Majority Opinion:	Justice Tom C. Clark
	367 U.S. 643
	laws.findlaw.com/US/367/643.html

DECISION

Evidence obtained by searches and seizures that were conducted in violation of the Constitution's Fourth Amendment is inadmissible in a criminal trial in a state court. The Court extended the so-called exclusionary rule, previously applied only to federal criminal prosecutions, to state courts.

BACKGROUND

In 1914 the Supreme Court ruled in *Weeks v. United States* that when police use illegal means to obtain evidence against a criminal suspect, that evidence cannot be used against the suspect at trial in a federal court. Without such a rule, the *Weeks* Court found, "The protection of the Fourth Amendment declaring [a defendant's] right to be secure against such searches and seizures is of no value, and, so far as those thus placed are concerned, might as well be stricken from the Constitution."

At the federal level, the exclusionary rule was viewed as an effective way to encourage law enforcement officials to abide by the Fourth Amendment in conducting searches and seizures. If police abuses resulted in the evidence being tossed out at trial, the theory went, then police would think twice about conducting illegal searches. As Judge Benjamin Cardozo put it in a New York case, "The criminal is to go free because the constable has blundered."

But in a series of decisions since *Weeks*, the Court had resisted efforts to extend the rule to state courts, which is, after all, where most people encounter the criminal justice system. The Court argued that the Bill of Rights governed only federal action. As recently as 1949, the Court in *Wolf v. Colorado* had found that state courts did not have to exclude illegally obtained evidence from trials, even though the Fourth Amendment's protection against illegal searches applied to local police as well as to federal agents. Gradually, however, the Court began to "incorporate" the states into protections of other parts of the Bill of Rights such as the First Amendment, by way of the Fourteenth Amendment, which did affect state action.

Indeed, the case that came to the Court appeared to involve a First Amendment issue, not evidence. It concerned a 1957 search by Cleveland police of the apartment of Dollree Mapp, suspected of involvement in an illegal gambling operation. She resisted and asked to see a search warrant. When police waved a piece of paper in front of her, she snatched it and put it down the front of her blouse. Police fought to get it back, and it is not entirely clear whether it was in fact a valid search warrant. None was produced at the trial.

Police proceeded to search the apartment in what the Supreme Court characterized as a "highhanded manner." They found no evidence of gambling, but did find some allegedly obscene literature and photographs in a locked suitcase. Mapp claimed the suitcase belonged to a former boarder, but she was convicted of possessing pornography and sentenced to prison for up to seven years. On appeal, the Ohio Supreme Court ruled that under Ohio law the results of the search were admissible, even though the search was unlawful. Mapp's conviction was upheld.

When the case came to the Supreme Court, Mapp's lawyers argued that the Ohio obscenity law was unconstitutionally vague. A friend-of-the-court brief by the American Civil Liberties Union argued that the evidence should be excluded because it was illegally obtained, but that issue was barely mentioned in oral arguments.

Dollree Mapp, Ohioan appealing conviction for pornography possession.
Courtesy of the Cleveland Press Collection

As recounted in a biography of Earl Warren by Ed Cray, a majority of the justices agreed in private conference to overturn Mapp's conviction on First Amendment grounds. Chief Justice Warren and Justices Douglas and Brennan indicated they also wanted to reverse the conviction on Fourth Amendment grounds, but no other justices appeared to support them, and the idea was dropped. Then, in a casual conversation in a Court elevator, Justice Clark told Brennan and Black that *Mapp* could be the vehicle for applying the Fourth Amendment exclusionary rule to the states. They agreed, and Clark wrote the opinion to include that point. Justice Frankfurter, who had written the Court's opinion in *Wolf,* was furious when he saw Clark's draft opinion. He argued that the Fourth Amendment issue had not been fully argued and should not be ruled on. But he did not prevail.

VOTE

5-4, with Justice Tom C. Clark writing for the majority. Joining in the majority were Chief Justice Earl Warren and Justices William O. Douglas, William J. Brennan Jr., and Hugo L. Black. Dissenting were Justices John M. Harlan, Felix Frankfurter, Charles E. Whittaker, and Potter Stewart.

HIGHLIGHTS

Justice Clark's main argument was that if the exclusionary rule was an effective constitutional rule at the federal level, it would be illogical, given the Fourteenth Amendment, not to extend the rule to state-conducted searches as well. "Presently, a federal prosecutor may make no use of evidence illegally seized, but a State's attorney across the street may, although he supposedly is operating under the enforceable prohibitions of the same Amendment," Clark wrote.

Recalling Cardozo's statement, Clark wrote, "The criminal goes free, if he must, but it is the law that sets him free. Nothing can destroy a government more quickly than its failure to observe its own laws, or worse, its disregard of the charter of its own existence."

Justice Black reached the same conclusion in his concurring opinion, but through the Fourth and Fifth Amendments in tandem, not the Fourteenth.

Justice Harlan's dissent clung to the old arguments against applying the Bill of Rights to actions by the states and accused the majority of abandoning "judicial restraint." The majority's view, Harlan said, "disfigures the boundaries" between the federal and state governments.

EXCERPTS

From Justice Clark's majority opinion: "Having once recognized that the right to privacy embodied in the Fourth Amendment is enforceable against the States, and that the right to be secure against rude invasions of privacy by state officers is, therefore, constitutional in origin, we can no longer permit that right to remain an empty promise. Because it is enforceable in the same manner and to like effect as other basic rights secured by the Due Process Clause, we can no longer permit it to be revocable at the whim of any police officer who, in the name of law enforcement itself, chooses to suspend its enjoyment. Our decision, founded on reason and truth, gives to the individual no more than that which the Constitution guarantees him, to the police officer no less than that to which honest law enforcement is entitled, and, to the Courts, that judicial integrity so necessary in the true administration of justice."

IMPACT

Justice Clark's offhand remark in an elevator transformed a minor First Amendment case into one of the Warren Court's most significant criminal law decisions. Along with *Gideon v. Wainwright* and *Miranda v. Arizona*, *Mapp* transformed police practices nationwide. Later Chief Justice Warren said of *Mapp*, "It's hard to say it's a case. It's like a huge cloud from which a lot of things are raining."

Even though the idea of exclusionary rule originated in the *Weeks* case, *Mapp* is far better known and more controversial because it applied the rule to a far broader range of cases. To critics, it exemplified the Warren Court's liberal concern for the rights of defendants as opposed to the needs of law enforcement. Critics and defenders disagree over the impact of *Mapp* on prosecutions, but in 1983 one study indicated that fewer than three percent of felony prosecutions were spoiled by improper searches that led to the exclusion of evidence.

As the Court pendulum swung back toward more conservative decisions, *Mapp* came under steady attack. Warren Burger, named by President Richard Nixon to succeed Chief Justice Warren, was critical of *Mapp*, and during the 1970s and 1980s the Court weakened it. In a pair of decisions in 1984, for example, the Court said illegally obtained evidence could be admitted at trial if it could be shown that police would have "inevitably" discovered it without the illegal search, or that police were acting in good faith based on a defective search warrant.

In *Herring v. United States*, a 2009 case, Chief Justice Roberts wrote a decision that critics said also weakened the exclusionary rule. It said that when police conduct an illegal search caused by "isolated negligence" such as a clerical error, the rule does not apply and the evidence obtained by police can be used at trial.

As for Dollree Mapp, described by some as "the Rosa Parks of the Fourth Amendment," she moved to New York where she was convicted in 1974 on charges of selling narcotics. She was sentenced to twenty years to life in prison, but in 1980 her sentence was commuted. Mapp died in Georgia in 2014 at the age of 91.

BAKER v. CARR

Subject:	Voting rights
Decided:	March 26, 1962
Chief Justice:	Earl Warren (R, Eisenhower appointee)
Petitioner:	Charles W. Baker, leader of a group of Tennessee voters
Respondent:	Joseph Carr, Tennessee secretary of state
Vote:	6-2 for Baker
Majority Opinion:	Justice William J. Brennan Jr.
	369 U.S. 186
	laws.findlaw.com/US/369/186.html

DECISION

Disputes over reapportionment — the drawing of election district boundaries — can be considered by federal courts. Earlier decisions saying that federal courts should stay away from "political questions" such as reapportionment are wrong. The Constitution specifically gives Congress the power to regulate the "times, places or manner" of electing senators and representatives. In addition, reapportionment has implications for the "equal protection of the laws" guaranteed to individuals by the Fourteenth Amendment to the Constitution. As a result, reapportionment is an appropriate subject for federal courts to address.

BACKGROUND

When legislative districts contain roughly equal numbers of people, the voting power of the people is also equal. For example, if two districts have approximately 100,000 voters within their boundaries, each individual has roughly the same say in electing the representatives from those districts. But what happens when the population shifts, and one district has 200,000 voters and the next district contains only 50,000? In such a case, a voter in the more populous district has less political power than a voter in the less-populated district.

Such disparities resulted from the migration of large numbers of Americans from rural to urban areas in the early twentieth century, without major changes in election district boundaries. In 1920, for the first time, census figures showed that more Americans lived in urban than rural settings. But for forty more years, lawmakers in many states refused to redraw legislative district boundaries to reflect those changes. Rural interests thereby gained disproportionately greater power in many state legislatures.

Urban interests sought to correct the imbalance, but legislators and the courts turned them down. In *Colegrove v. Green* the Supreme Court in 1946 ruled that the courts should stay out of an Illinois dispute over legislative districts in which the disparity between districts was as high as 800,000 people. "Courts ought not to enter this political thicket," Justice Felix Frankfurter wrote, coining a phrase that is still used by the courts. "It is hostile to a democratic system to involve the judiciary in the politics of the people."

The Court had shut the door on deciding these cases, but problems continued to grow. Los Angeles, California, had one state senator for its six million residents, while another California district, with around 14,000 residents, also elected a state senator. Such disparities extended to the congressional districts.

In the view of some political scientists, these disparities were not just abstract problems; rather, they had real-life consequences. State legislatures and Congress were paying scant attention during this period to urban issues — housing and welfare, for example — as well as issues of race, and the dominance of rural interests in state legislatures was partly to blame. It was probably inevitable that the issue would return to the Supreme Court. A case from Tennessee provided an opportunity for the Court to revisit it.

Between 1901 and 1961 the Tennessee legislature had resisted all efforts to change its legislative districts, even though the state had experienced the same shift in population to urban areas that was occurring in other states. Rural residents exercised far more power over state legislative matters than their urban counterparts. By 1960 this disparity reached the point where roughly two-thirds of the state representatives were being elected by one-third of the state's 3.6 million people.

The Tennessee courts were also unsympathetic, ruling that they, like the federal courts, had no power to meddle in what were essentially political determinations about district boundaries. Finally, a group of voters from Memphis, Nashville, and Knoxville led by Charles W. Baker went to federal court with a lawsuit against Joseph Carr, the Tennessee secretary of state. The voters claimed that the disparity in districts reflected an "unconstitutional and obsolete" system that denied them equal protection of the laws. The district court, relying on the Supreme Court's precedents, said federal courts had no jurisdiction over the issues raised in the suit and that those issues were "nonjusticiable," meaning that they were not appropriate for judicial determination.

VOTE

6-2, with Justice William J. Brennan Jr. writing the majority opinion. Joining Brennan were Chief Justice Earl Warren and Justices Hugo L. Black, William O. Douglas, Tom C. Clark, and Potter Stewart. Justices Felix Frankfurter and John M. Harlan dissented. Justice Charles E. Whittaker did not participate.

HIGHLIGHTS

The Supreme Court, by all accounts, struggled with this case. It heard three hours of oral argument on the case during one term and then rescheduled it for another three hours in the next. Justice Clark, in a concurring opinion, said the case "has been most carefully considered over and over again by us in Conference and individually." According to Court historians, in internal deliberations the majority was frequently in doubt. It was not until the last moment that it became a 6-2 decision, when Clark changed his mind and voted with the majority.

When the opinion was finally issued, the various writings — three concurring opinions and two dissents, in addition to the main opinion — totaled 163 pages. Frankfurter's dissent, which proved to be his last major opinion, was sixty-four pages. Frankfurter angrily called the majority opinion a "massive repudiation of the experience of our whole past" because it thrust the federal courts into the political realm.

But to Justice Brennan, the result seemed obvious. He avoided the actual merits of the Tennessee case, focusing instead on the threshold question of whether the courts had jurisdiction and the issues involved could be resolved judicially. He said federal courts have jurisdiction because the lawsuit "arises under" a part of the Constitution, namely the Fourteenth Amendment. He also found that the plaintiffs in the case had "standing" — the right to sue — because their right to vote was at stake.

The pivotal part of the ruling was the determination that the issue was "justiciable," which is different from the question of whether the Court has jurisdiction. For a dispute to be justiciable, the Court has to be able to identify the problem and fashion a remedy that it has the right to impose, using manageable standards to make the determination.

In prior cases the Court had decided that two types of disputes were not justiciable: those involving "political questions" and claims that rely on the Guaranty Clause of the Constitution, under which the federal government guarantees a republican form of government to all states. Brennan swept those obstacles aside, narrowing the definition of political questions that the Court must avoid. Because resolving *Baker v. Carr* did not require the Court to impinge on the separation of powers or to make political judgments, Brennan found the case justiciable. His opinion gave short shrift to the Guaranty Clause, finding that the Fourteenth Amendment's Equal Protection Clause was a valid ground for bringing a reapportionment lawsuit.

EXCERPTS

From Justice Brennan's majority opinion: "Of course, the mere fact that the suit seeks protection of a political right does not mean it presents a political question. Such an objection 'is little more than a play upon words.' Rather, it is argued that apportionment cases, whatever the actual wording of the complaint, can involve no federal constitutional right except one resting on the guaranty of a republican form of government, and that complaints based on that clause have been held to present political questions which are nonjusticiable.

"We hold that the claim pleaded here neither rests upon nor implicates the Guaranty Clause and that its justiciability is therefore not foreclosed by our decisions of cases involving that clause. The District Court misinterpreted *Colegrove v. Green* and other decisions of this Court on which it relied. Appellants' claim that they are being denied equal protection is justiciable.... .

"We conclude that the complaint's allegations of a denial of equal protection present a justiciable constitutional cause of action upon which appellants are entitled to a trial and a decision. The right asserted is within the reach of judicial protection under the Fourteenth Amendment."

IMPACT

The Court's decision is often associated with the phrase "one person, one vote," which actually did not appear in its text. That standard was announced a year later in *Gray v. Sanders*, a case that built on *Baker*. The Court in *Gray v. Sanders* struck down Georgia's "county unit" system of electing state officials because rural counties had more weight than urban counties.

Still, the sweep of *Baker v. Carr* would be difficult to overstate. Chief Justice Warren said in his memoirs that the case was "the most important case of my tenure on the Court" — no small statement from the man who wrote the Court's ruling in *Brown v. Board of Education*.

By the end of 1962, more than sixty lawsuits had been initiated, and a dozen state legislatures had met, all with the goal of reapportioning districts to achieve more equal representation. Gradually the nation's electoral map was redrawn, shifting the balance of power toward urban areas and away from rural interests. Reapportionment after every decennial census, only spottily done before the decision, has become routine because of the ruling. The Court has continued to grapple with reapportionment cases ever since, especially on the question of redrawing districts to concentrate the voting power of minorities.

Baker v. Carr has been identified as a major milestone on the Court's road toward greater activism. Frankfurter's view that judges should shy away from the "political thicket" was replaced by Brennan's view that courts had a responsibility to vindicate constitutional rights, even in areas once viewed as off-limits. It was one of several decisions in which the liberal Brennan sought to give individuals greater access to the courts in the interest of freedom and justice.

The *Baker* decision played a prominent role in the Court's 2004 decision *Vieth v. Jubelirer*, involving the politically motivated redistricting of Pennsylvania congressional districts after the 2000 census. In a 1986 case *Davis v. Bandemer*, the Court had said courts could scrutinize claims of political gerrymandering, but in the years after that ruling, lower courts struggled to find the proper standard for reviewing such political determinations.

In *Vieth*, four justices said the courts should just abandon the enterprise, because the *Baker v. Carr* requirement that there be "manageable standards" for deciding political gerrymandering cases could not be met. Justice Anthony Kennedy, in the decisive fifth vote, said the door should not be closed permanently on the possibility of finding the proper standard under *Baker v. Carr*. But he agreed with the other four justices in the majority that in this case, the Democratic challenge to the Republican-controlled Pennsylvania redistricting should be dismissed.

In the fall of 2015, the Court hears arguments in a case that relates closely to the "one person one vote" doctrine. In *Evenwel v. Abbott*, a group of Texas voters is asking the justices to decide whether, in creating equal districts, states must count total population or just registered voters. They claim that if total population is used, the small number of voters in urban districts with a high percentage of non-voters end up having relatively more political clout than the larger number of voters in rural districts where fewer non-voters live. In short, a smaller number of voters in one district can control outcomes than in another district, even though the population in both districts is roughly the same.

In a 2001 case, Justice Thomas signaled his interest in resolving this question. "We have never determined the relevant 'population' that states and localities must equally distribute among their districts," he wrote. "As long as we sustain the one-person-one-vote principle, we have an obligation to explain to states and localities what it actually means."

*Justice William J. Brennan Jr., author of the
majority opinion.* Source: Library of Congress

Chief Justice Earl Warren, author of the
majority opinion. Source: Library of Congress

MIRANDA v. ARIZONA

Subject:	Right to counsel
Decided:	June 13, 1966
Chief Justice:	Earl Warren (R, Eisenhower appointee)
Petitioner:	Ernesto Miranda, Arizonan appealing conviction for kidnapping and rape
Respondent:	State of Arizona
Vote:	5-4 for Miranda
Majority Opinion:	Chief Justice Earl Warren
	384 U.S. 436
	laws.findlaw.com/US/384/436.html

DECISION

The Fifth Amendment protects individuals against being forced to make statements that will help the government prove that they committed a crime. Before suspects in police custody can be questioned, they must be informed that they have the right to remain silent, that anything they say may be used against them, that they have the right to have a lawyer present, as well as the right to have a lawyer appointed to defend them if they cannot afford a lawyer.

BACKGROUND

In writing the Bill of Rights the Framers, who had grown to despise the abusive practices of British criminal prosecutions, placed great emphasis on the rights of the criminally accused.

It is no accident, then, that four of the first ten amendments to the Constitution deal with the rights of the accused. The Fifth Amendment states, "No person… shall be compelled in any criminal case to be a witness against himself." Just how that rule should be enforced has been the subject of dozens of Supreme Court cases. At the end of the nineteenth century, the Court said that for confessions to be admissible in federal court they had to have been given "freely and voluntarily." In 1936 that rule was extended to state cases. The determination of whether a confession was voluntary was made on a case-by-case basis. As a result, cases involving confessions continued to appear on the Court's docket, some of them clearly indicating that police were using "third degree" tactics during interrogations. Justices began to look for cases that would enable the Court to announce a clearer rule for determining if a confession was voluntary.

Two decisions by the Court applying the Sixth Amendment right to the "assistance of counsel" hastened the search. In *Gideon v. Wainwright* in 1963, the Court ruled that the right to have the assistance of a lawyer was fundamental for anyone accused of a felony. A year later, in *Escobedo v. Illinois*, the Court ruled that if police do not inform a suspect of his right to remain silent, and if they deny the suspect's request to speak with his lawyer, his Sixth Amendment rights have been violated. The defendant in the case, Danny Escobedo, had been questioned for fourteen hours in connection with the murder of his brother-in-law. The Court reversed his conviction.

The *Escobedo* decision applied mainly to cases in which a defendant already had a lawyer. According to a biographer, Chief Justice Warren felt that "more needed to be said" about the issues raised in *Escobedo*. He asked his law clerks to look for appropriate cases among the 170 that had come to the Court since *Escobedo* raising issues about confessions. Ernesto Miranda's case provided the Chief with the vehicle he was seeking.

Ernesto Miranda was twenty-three years old when he was arrested in 1963 in Phoenix as a suspect in the kidnapping and rape of a young woman. The victim's 1953 Packard was parked in front of his house, and he matched the general description the woman gave police of her attacker. The victim identified Miranda in a police lineup. In addition, Miranda had a history of arrests for rape and "Peeping Tom" offenses.

Miranda at first denied any involvement in the rape, but by the end of two hours of questioning by police, he confessed. He signed a statement that included a standard paragraph stating that the confession was voluntarily given. But Miranda had not been told that he had the right to have an attorney present or that he had the right to remain silent. At trial, his lawyer said the confession should not be admitted into evidence, but it was, and Miranda was convicted and sentenced to twenty years in prison. He appealed.

At oral argument before the Supreme Court, Miranda's lawyer conceded the confession had not been coerced, but insisted that Miranda had given up a right that he did not fully appreciate or understand. The Supreme Court was sharply divided over the case, with some justices fearing that any ruling restricting police behavior during interrogations would hamper the police. But Chief Justice Warren, who had once been a district attorney in California, argued forcefully that reform was needed. He noted that he had ordered law enforcement officials in his jurisdiction to warn suspects of their rights against forced self-incrimination. Other justices were also swayed by the fact that the Federal Bureau of Investigation (FBI) and District of Columbia police routinely gave the warnings.

VOTE

5-4, with Chief Justice Earl Warren writing the majority opinion. He was joined by Justices Hugo L. Black, William O. Douglas, William J. Brennan Jr., and Abe Fortas. Justices Tom C. Clark, John M. Harlan, Byron R. White, and Potter Stewart dissented.

HIGHLIGHTS

Supreme Court rulings are often written in ways that provide lower court judges and the general public with few clear rules about how to proceed. Not so with *Miranda*, which speaks boldly and clearly to prosecutors, police, and the public alike. Moreover, the Court normally is inclined to lay down general rules that can be applied with some flexibility to individual situations. But in *Miranda*, the Court said unequivocally that what has come to be known as the Miranda warning is an "absolute prerequisite" for the admissibility of confessions.

"The Fifth Amendment privilege is so fundamental to our system of constitutional rule and the expedient of giving an adequate warning as to the availability of the privilege so simple, we will not pause to inquire in individual cases whether the defendant was aware of his rights without a warning being given," Chief Justice Warren wrote.

The opinion recites the history of the law regarding confessions, as well as established practices within the FBI and in other countries, to reassure the public that its clear rule is neither new nor particularly onerous. In Scotland and India, for example, nearly all confessions made under police interrogation have long been excluded.

While giving Congress and the states some leeway to devise procedures for implementing its rule, the Court said any procedure had to include a warning with four basic elements: You have the right to remain silent; anything you say can and will be used against you; you have the right to talk to a lawyer and have the lawyer present during questioning; if you cannot afford a lawyer, one will be provided to you before questioning can begin.

The opinion also takes pains to spell out when the Miranda rule comes into play. The Court says that police may investigate and ask questions at a crime scene without reading anyone the Miranda warning. But once an individual has been taken into custody "or otherwise deprived of his freedom of action in any significant way," the warning must be given.

That point at which the warning must be given is substantially earlier than police wanted. Some asserted that the Fifth Amendment privilege applies only when an individual is questioned in court or in some other kind of official proceeding. But the Supreme Court in *Miranda* said in vivid terms that the protection against self-incrimination must be invoked at the custody stage to have any force at all.

"An individual swept from familiar surroundings into police custody, surrounded by antagonistic forces, and subjected to the techniques of persuasion ... cannot be otherwise than under compulsion to speak," the Court said.

EXCERPTS

From Chief Justice Warren's majority opinion: "The current practice of incommunicado interrogation is at odds with one of our Nation's most cherished principles — that the individual may not be compelled to incriminate himself. Unless adequate protective devices are employed to dispel the compulsion inherent in custodial surroundings, no statement obtained from the defendant can truly be the product of his free choice.... .

"... [T]he privilege against self-incrimination — the essential mainstay of our adversary system — is founded on a complex of values. All these policies point to one overriding thought: the constitutional foundation underlying the privilege is the respect a government — state or federal — must accord to the dignity and integrity of its citizens. To maintain a 'fair state-individual balance,' to require the government 'to shoulder the entire load,' to respect the inviolability of the human personality, our accusatory system of criminal justice demands that the government seeking to punish an individual produce the evidence against him by its own independent labors, rather than by the cruel, simple expedient of compelling it from his own mouth.... .

"Accordingly, we hold that an individual held for interrogation must be clearly informed that he has the right to consult with a lawyer and to have the lawyer with him during interrogation under the system for protecting the privilege we delineate today. As with the warnings of the right to remain silent and that anything stated can be used in evidence against him, this warning is an absolute prerequisite to interrogation. No amount of circumstantial evidence that the person may have been aware of this right will suffice to stand in its stead: only through such a warning is there ascertainable assurance that the accused was aware of this right."

IMPACT

In the decades since *Miranda v. Arizona*, the so-called Miranda warning became familiar to the public, thanks to countless television police shows and movies in which police recite the admonition to arrestees. The decision also remained controversial. Law enforcement officials and political conservatives attacked it as giving too much weight to the rights of criminal defendants while ignoring the interests of police and crime victims in determining the truth.

In 1968 Congress passed a law aimed at overturning *Miranda*. It allowed confessions to be admitted in federal cases, even if they were made without Miranda warnings, so long as it could be shown that they were voluntary. But the Justice Department consistently declined to enforce the law, believing that *Miranda* took precedence. Critics of *Miranda* began invoking the dormant law in court cases, however, in hopes that the Supreme Court would uphold the law and effectively nullify its decision.

In 2000 the Court ruled on the issue in the case of *Dickerson v. United States*. By a 7-2 vote the Court said the *Miranda* decision had constitutional dimensions and took precedence over the federal law. Surprisingly Chief Justice William Rehnquist, a longtime critic of *Miranda*, wrote the Dickerson opinion upholding it. In part, his ruling was a statement of the Court's authority, telling Congress that the Supreme Court, not Congress, decides the meaning of the Constitution. But Rehnquist also recognized how much the Miranda decision had become accepted by police and by society. "Miranda has become embedded in routine police practice to the point where the warnings have become part of our national culture," Rehnquist wrote.

Some commentators minimized the importance of *Dickerson*, asserting that the Miranda rule had already been considerably weakened. In the years since *Miranda*, the Supreme Court in numerous decisions has chipped away at it by allowing police some leeway to make mistakes in interrogations and requiring suspects to explicitly invoke their right to remain silent.

A 2013 Supreme Court ruling exemplified the ways in which the Miranda rule has been watered down. In *Salinas v. Texas*, murder suspect Genovevo Salinas was interviewed by police without having been given the Miranda warning. He answered some questions but fell silent when an officer asked him if a ballistics test would show that shell casings at the murder scene would match his shotgun. At trial, prosecutors pointed to his silence as a sign of his guilt. By a 5-4 vote, the Supreme Court said Salinas's Fifth Amendment rights had not been violated because he did not explicitly invoke his privilege against forced self-incrimination.

Nonetheless, the Court has not repudiated *Miranda* altogether, and it remains as a deeply entrenched procedural rule for police.

Legal scholars dispute *Miranda*'s impact on the ability of police to solve crimes. Paul Cassell of the University of Utah, who argued in *Dickerson*, contended that thousands of criminal cases go unsolved every year because the Miranda rule caused confessions to be tossed out or because suspects refused to talk. Other researchers say the impact is vastly overstated.

Many police officials say they have learned to live with — or even embrace — the Miranda rule. Some say it has helped police nationwide become more professional, with higher standards of ethics and fairness.

Others even suggest that *Miranda* has given police an extra measure of credibility when defendants confess. A substantial percentage of suspects who are given Miranda warnings waive their right to remain silent and continue to talk to police. If the suspect has signed a Miranda waiver, any subsequent confession can be placed into evidence with relative ease.

Critics of police practices say many officers have also developed ways of getting around *Miranda* by, for example, advising suspects of their rights, but then telling them they would be better off if they talked.

Ernesto Miranda himself was tried and convicted again, this time without using the confession against him. He was imprisoned until 1972 and went back to prison in 1975 after another run-in with the law. After he was released, Miranda in 1976 was murdered in a fight at a Phoenix bar. According to some reports, he had several "Miranda cards," reciting the police warning his case had inspired, in his pocket when he died.

Plaintiff Norma McCorvey, known as "Jane Roe" in Roe v. Wade.
Photo by Cynthia Johnson/The LIFE Images Collection/Getty Images

ROE v. WADE

Subject:	Abortion rights
Decided:	January 22, 1973
Chief Justice:	Warren E. Burger (R, Nixon appointee)
Petitioner:	"Jane Roe" (Norma McCorvey), a Texas woman seeking an abortion
Respondent:	Henry Wade, Dallas County district attorney
Vote:	7-2 for Roe
Majority Opinion:	Justice Harry A. Blackmun
	410 U.S. 113
	laws.findlaw.com/US/410/113.html

DECISION

A woman's right to an abortion is part of her constitutionally protected right of privacy under the Fourteenth Amendment, although the right is not absolute. Before the end of the first trimester, the decision to abort must be left to the pregnant woman and her physician. During the second trimester, the state may regulate abortion "in ways that are reasonably related to maternal health." Once the fetus is viable, government may restrict or even prohibit abortion, except to preserve the life or health of the mother.

BACKGROUND

The question of abortion — whether and when a woman has the right to end a pregnancy — is one of the most divisive issues ever to come before the Supreme Court. It tests moral, legal, and medical principles in ways that rarely produce easy answers or calm debate. *Abortion: The Clash of Absolutes* is the apt name of a book on the subject by Harvard law professor Laurence Tribe.

For most of U.S. history, however, abortion was not a major issue. "Abortion, at least early in pregnancy, was neither prohibited nor uncommon," writes Tribe. Under common law, abortion was permitted before "quickening," the point when the pregnant woman feels movement by the fetus for the first time — usually the fourth or fifth month of pregnancy.

The push to enact laws restricting abortions came in the nineteenth century, not from religious leaders but from the medical profession. Some have said that doctors were trying to discourage competition from the growing number of abortionists, but other historians claim the motivation was to increase the professionalism of medical practitioners. Doctors also note that the Hippocratic Oath, which guides their profession, bars doctors from giving women a "pessary to produce abortion." The first laws made abortions before quickening a lesser crime than abortions performed after that point, and allowed physicians to make exceptions when the mother's life was endangered.

By the mid-twentieth century most of those laws had been tightened, and abortion was made broadly illegal, driving the procedure underground. Debate over these laws was revived in the 1960s in part by a rubella epidemic and a highly publicized controversy over so-called thalidomide babies. Rubella or German measles in pregnant women resulted in birth defects for the child, and the use of the tranquilizer thalidomide by mothers produced babies with severe deformities. Sherri Finkbine, a mother who had taken thalidomide before its damaging effects were made public, had to travel to Sweden to get an abortion after a front-page controversy over whether she should be able to have an abortion in the United States. Both episodes, according to Tribe, triggered a reexamination of the issue by doctors and the public. In 1967 the American Medical Association called for the liberalization of abortion laws to allow a greater range of exceptions to bans on the practice.

At the same time, legal doctrines were evolving that encouraged a court challenge to laws restricting abortion. The Court's 1965 decision in *Griswold v. Connecticut*, in particular, tied together several other precedents to assert a personal right of privacy grounded in different parts of the Constitution. The decision struck down a state law banning the use of contraceptives, even by married couples. That right of privacy, the Court said, shielded a range of personal decisions from intrusion by government. In the book *Liberty and Sexuality*, the definitive work on the issue, author David Garrow suggests that without the *Griswold* decision, the Supreme Court would not have declared a constitutional right to have an abortion.

Abortion rights groups in several states began looking for plaintiffs to make a test case of whether antiabortion laws violated women's constitutional rights. Texas lawyers Linda Coffee and Sarah Weddington found a willing plaintiff in Norma McCorvey. She was an unmarried Dallas carnival worker who wanted an abortion because she could not afford to raise a child. Her desperate search for a way to end the pregnancy led her to the lawyers, and she readily agreed to participate in a suit against the Texas abortion ban, which dated back to 1854. She told the lawyers she had been raped, but years later she said that was not true.

According to her book *I Am Roe*, McCorvey mistakenly believed the lawsuit could be resolved in time for her to have an abortion. "It would be nice to say," she said in the book, "that ... I realized I was making abortion-rights history. Or changing my life forever. But the honest truth is that nothing like that even occurred to me. I was simply at the end of my rope." Her only request was that she be allowed to remain anonymous, which is why the lawsuit listed her as "Jane Roe." The suit, filed in early 1970, listed Dallas County District Attorney Henry Wade as the defendant because it was his job to enforce the abortion law in Dallas.

A three-judge panel sided with McCorvey, striking down the Texas law and declaring that the "fundamental right of single women and married persons to choose whether to have children is protected by the Ninth Amendment, through the Fourteenth Amendment." The rarely cited Ninth Amendment reserves to the people those rights not specifically listed in the Constitution. As the case proceeded, McCorvey gave birth to the child and put it up for adoption.

The Texas case, along with a challenge to Georgia's abortion law, arrived at the Supreme Court at an awkward time. Only seven justices were available to consider it. New justices Lewis F. Powell Jr. and William H. Rehnquist had been confirmed, but not sworn in by the time of oral argument. After oral arguments, Chief Justice Burger assigned the drafting of an opinion to Justice Blackmun, one-time legal counsel to the famed Mayo Clinic. Blackmun toiled for months on the decision, finally sending a draft to his colleagues in May. The draft opinion asserted that the Texas law was unconstitutionally vague. But after several justices suggested the ruling needed to be beefed up, Blackmun urged that it be reargued in the fall, allowing the new justices to participate. He then spent several weeks that summer in the medical library at the Mayo Clinic researching the history of abortion.

Following the second argument in the case, Blackmun produced a stronger draft that reflected his research. With some significant further revisions, the Court's historic ruling was released.

VOTE

7-2, with Justice Harry A. Blackmun writing the opinion of the Court. Joining Blackmun were Chief Justice Warren E. Burger, William O. Douglas, William J. Brennan Jr., Potter Stewart, Thurgood Marshall, and Lewis F. Powell Jr. Dissenting were Justices Byron R. White and William H. Rehnquist.

HIGHLIGHTS

In major constitutional cases, the Court often gives great weight to how the issue involved was handled at the time of the drafting of the Constitution and relevant constitutional amendments. Heeding that practice, Justice Blackmun spent considerable time in the opinion reviewing the history of abortion in the United States. The history bolstered the Court's main decision in favor of a constitutional right to an abortion.

Blackmun wrote, "At common law, at the time of the adoption of our Constitution, and throughout the major portion of the 19th century, abortion was viewed with less disfavor than under most American statutes currently in effect. Phrasing it another way, a woman enjoyed a substantially broader right to terminate a pregnancy than she does in most States today. At least with respect to the early stage of pregnancy, and very possibly without such a limitation, the opportunity to make this choice was present in this country well into the 19th century."

As a preliminary issue, Blackmun also dealt with the touchy question of whether a fetus was a "person" under the Fourteenth Amendment, which guarantees due process and equal protection for "persons born or naturalized in the United States." In Blackmun's view, a fetus was not a person. "The Constitution does not define 'person' in so many words," Blackmun wrote. He then reviewed all the instances in which the word person appears in the Constitution. "All this, together with our observation that throughout the major portion of the 19th century prevailing legal abortion practices were far freer than they are today, persuades us that the word 'person,' as used in the Fourteenth Amendment, does not include the unborn."

Blackmun stayed away from another thorny issue. "We need not resolve the difficult question of when life begins. When those trained in the respective disciplines of medicine, philosophy, and theology are unable to arrive at any consensus, the judiciary, at this point in the development of man's knowledge, is not in a position to speculate as to the answer."

The pregnant woman, Blackmun asserted, has a fundamental right to privacy under *Griswold* and other Court rulings, and making the decision whether to carry a child to birth is part of that right. But that right is not absolute, Blackmun argued; at some point in the pregnancy the state's interest in protecting public health and human lives justifies state regulation or even prohibition of abortions. Because abortions are more dangerous to the woman the later in pregnancy they occur, protecting the health of the woman, as well as the life of the fetus, comes into play.

But determining the point when government intervention becomes constitutional was difficult. In earlier drafts of the decision, according to Garrow, Blackmun fixed it at the end of the first trimester — three months into pregnancy. Other justices felt that was too early in the pregnancy and feared that if the Court drew the line there, states would prohibit abortions after the first trimester, leaving the rights of many women unprotected.

Blackmun agreed to modify the approach. He kept his reference to the first trimester, noting that up to that point, the abortion procedure is safer in terms of the woman's health than childbirth. After that point, regulations that "reasonably relate" to the mother's health are permitted.

The point at which state interests in the fetus become compelling, Blackmun said, is "viability" — when the fetus could live outside the mother's womb. Blackmun did not say when viability is reached, but at the time it was regarded as being somewhere near the end of the second trimester. After viability, states could regulate or even ban abortions, except to protect the life or health of the mother. In between these two points, Blackmun suggested, the states would have some flexibility in devising regulations.

The dissenters argued that the majority opinion had invented a right not contained in the Constitution, and had artificially divided a woman's pregnancy into three parts. If the state had a legitimate interest in fetal health, they reasoned, the interest should last through the entire pregnancy, not just the last third.

Justice White's dissent struck a bitter tone. "The Court, for the most part, sustains this position: during the period prior to the time the fetus becomes viable, the Constitution of the United States values the convenience, whim, or caprice of the putative mother more than the life or potential life of the fetus."

Justice Rehnquist also wrote a dissent, "The decision here to break pregnancy into three distinct terms and to outline the permissible restrictions the State may impose in each one … partakes more of judicial legislation than it does of a determination of the intent of the drafters of the Fourteenth Amendment."

In a second decision issued the same day, *Doe v. Bolton*, the Court also struck down Georgia's less restrictive abortion law.

EXCERPTS

From Justice Harry A. Blackmun's majority opinion: "We forthwith acknowledge our awareness of the sensitive and emotional nature of the abortion controversy, of the vigorous opposing views, even among physicians, and of the deep and seemingly absolute convictions that the subject inspires. One's philosophy, one's experiences, one's exposure to the raw edges of human existence, one's religious training, one's attitudes toward life and family and their values, and the moral standards one establishes and seeks to observe, are all likely to influence and to color one's thinking and conclusions about abortion.

"In addition, population growth, pollution, poverty, and racial overtones tend to complicate and not to simplify the problem.… .

"The Constitution does not explicitly mention any right of privacy. In a line of decisions, however, going back perhaps as far as *Union Pacific R. Co. v. Botsford* (1891), the Court has recognized that a right of personal privacy, or a guarantee of certain areas or zones of privacy, does exist under the Constitution.… . This right of privacy, whether it be founded in the Fourteenth Amendment's concept of personal liberty and restrictions upon state action, as we feel it is, or, as the District Court determined, in the Ninth Amendment's reservation of rights to the people, is broad enough to encompass a woman's decision whether or not to terminate her pregnancy.... .

"... The Court's decisions recognizing a right of privacy also acknowledge that some state regulation in areas protected by that right is appropriate.... . [A] State may properly assert important interests in safeguarding health, in maintaining medical standards, and in protecting potential life. At some point in pregnancy, these respective interests become sufficiently compelling to sustain regulation of the factors that govern the abortion decision. The privacy right involved, therefore, cannot be said to be absolute.... .

"With respect to the State's important and legitimate interest in the health of the mother, the 'compelling' point, in the light of present medical knowledge, is at approximately the end of the first trimester. This is so because of the now-established medical fact ... that, until the end of the first trimester mortality in abortion may be less than mortality in normal childbirth. It follows that, from and after this point, a State may regulate the abortion procedure to the extent that the regulation reasonably relates to the preservation and protection of maternal health. Examples of permissible state regulation in this area are requirements as to the qualifications of the person who is to perform the abortion; as to the licensure of that person; as to the facility in which the procedure is to be performed, that is, whether it must be a hospital or may be a clinic or some other place of less-than-hospital status; as to the licensing of the facility; and the like."

IMPACT

The initial reaction to the decision was muted in part because it was issued on the same day that former president Lyndon B. Johnson died, and his death dominated the headlines. Today, most scholars and historians agree that *Roe v. Wade* comes close to *Brown v. Board of Education* as one of the most important Supreme Court decisions of the twentieth century, if not the Court's entire history. The Court declared a constitutional right that had not existed before — a right that has had profound impact on society ever since.

Laws in virtually every state — except New York, which had already passed a law legalizing abortion — were invalidated overnight. Illegal abortions no longer were necessary, and the number of abortions soon totaled one-quarter of all pregnancies. Alan Guttmacher, president of the Planned Parenthood Federation of America, called *Roe* "a wise and courageous stroke for the right of privacy, and for the protection of a woman's physical and emotional health."

Women's rights advocates applauded the decision because it offered women, for the first time, substantial control over their reproductive lives. No longer would the course of women's lives, education, and careers be determined by an accidental or unwanted pregnancy.

For that same reason, many religious and political leaders bitterly attacked *Roe*. It cheapened human life, they said, making it too easy for women to extinguish a pregnancy if it seemed inconvenient at the moment. Close to one million abortions are performed every year in the United States according to the latest available statistics, though the number has declined over time, along with the decline in the number or teenage pregnancies. "It is hard to think of any decision in the 200 years of our history which has had more disastrous implications for our stability as a civilized society," said Philadelphia's Cardinal John Krol. Conservative columnist William F. Buckley called it "the Dred Scott decision of the twentieth century."

The decision has been criticized from a legal standpoint by conservatives and as a prime example of judicial activism — legislating from the bench without any firm grounding in the Constitution. Even some liberals have criticized *Roe v. Wade*. Ruth Bader Ginsburg, a women's rights lawyer who later joined the Court as a justice, said the Court "ventured too far" in its Roe ruling by deciding the issue broadly, thereby pre-empting the political process that might have allowed abortions through legislation state by state.

Rather than ending the abortion debate, *Roe* invigorated the "pro-life" movement that opposed abortion rights and transformed abortion into a wrenching political issue. It also brought the Supreme Court, more than ever before, into the political arena; demonstrations against the Court and especially against Justice Blackmun became routine.

Abortion cases became commonplace on the Court's docket, each one provoking controversy and, usually, a fragmented opinion from the Court that reflected its political leanings at the time. In 1976 the Court said the "father" of the fetus could not veto a woman's abortion choice. But in most cases since, the Court has approved of state legislative efforts to restrict the abortion right.

In *City of Akron v. Akron Center for Reproductive Health* (1983) the Court said states could require minors to obtain parental consent before they can have abortions, so long as there is an alternative procedure in cases where trying to obtain parental consent would endanger the pregnant young woman. Significantly in that case, the Court's first woman justice, Sandra Day O'Connor, indicated her misgivings about the *Roe* framework. Noting that medical advances had made fetuses viable outside the womb at earlier and earlier stages, she said the trimester framework of *Roe* was "on a collision course with itself."

In 1989 the appointment of conservative justices brought the Court close to overturning *Roe*. In *Webster v. Reproductive Health Services*, the Court by a 5-4 vote upheld several state restrictions on abortion. "A chill wind blows," Blackmun said in a dissent that warned of the possible demise of the abortion right. Blackmun's fears appeared to be somewhat premature. In 1992 the Bush administration explicitly asked the Court to overturn *Roe* in the case *Planned Parenthood of Southeastern Pennsylvania v. Casey*, which again involved state restrictions on abortion, including waiting periods and parental and spousal consent requirements. Surprisingly, the Court turned down the invitation and dramatically embraced *Roe's* holding.

A joint opinion by Justices O'Connor, David Souter, and Anthony Kennedy held in part that *Roe* had become embedded in the fabric of the nation and could not be jettisoned easily. "An entire generation has come of age free to assume *Roe's* concept of liberty in defining the capacity of women to act in society, and to make reproductive decisions," these justices wrote. "To overrule under fire in the absence of the most compelling reason to reexamine a watershed decision would subvert the Court's legitimacy beyond any serious question."

The decision used an "undue burden" standard in upholding most but not all parts of the Pennsylvania law. That standard, suggested by O'Connor in an earlier case asks whether a restriction on abortions places a "substantial obstacle in the path of a woman seeking an abortion" before the point of fetal viability.

In the years since the *Casey* decision, the Court has shown little appetite to revisit the abortion issue, except in the context of restrictions on the sometimes violent demonstrations that have taken place around abortion clinics. The Court has said some regulation of the demonstrations is permissible to protect the safety of patients and staff, but First

Amendment considerations make complete bans on such demonstrations unjustifiable.

But abortion rights opponents continued their campaign, urging Congress and the states to pass laws prohibiting what they called "partial-birth" abortions. Abortion rights advocates feared that, depending on how the procedure was defined, the law could cover operations that are fairly common. The Supreme Court in the 2000 ruling *Stenberg v. Carhart* struck down a Nebraska law prohibiting the procedure, in part because it did not make an exception from the ban if the health of the mother was at stake. Significantly, however, the Court's vote striking down the law was 5-4 with Justice Kennedy moving from the camp of abortion rights supporters to oppose the procedure.

In 2007, the Court upheld a federal law against partial-birth abortion that Congress passed in the wake of *Stenberg*, again by a 5-4 vote. The Court's newest justices — Chief Justice John Roberts Jr. and Justice Samuel Alito Jr. — voted with the majority in favor of the law.

The legal battle over abortion rights is far from over. Fueled in part by Republican victories at the state level, state legislatures in recent years have enacted a broad range of restrictions on abortions. The Guttmacher Institute said more than 200 laws restricting abortions have been enacted in 30 states since 2011. Many of the laws have targeted facilities where abortions take place, imposing hospital-like requirements that have led some clinics to shut down.

Not surprisingly, legal challenges to this new wave of restrictions are making their way back to the Supreme Court on appeal. The lawsuits claim that new restrictions fail the "undue burden" test by shuttering clinics and making it difficult for women in remote parts of the state to obtain abortions. These appeals may not directly threaten the future of the *Roe v. Wade* precedent, but the current lineup of justices suggests that at least some of the restrictions will be upheld.

APPENDICES

THE ROBERTS COURT

Chief Justice John G. Roberts Jr., 109th justice, 17th chief justice
Born: January 27, 1955; Buffalo, New York
Law school: Harvard Law School
Appointed by: President George W. Bush
Sworn in: September 29, 2005

Associate Justice Antonin Scalia, 103rd justice
Born: March 11, 1936; Trenton, New Jersey
Law school: Harvard Law School
Appointed by: President Ronald Reagan
Sworn in: September 26, 1986

Associate Justice Anthony M. Kennedy, 104th justice
Born: July 23, 1936; Sacramento, California
Law school: Harvard Law School
Appointed by: President Ronald Reagan
Sworn in: February 18, 1988

Associate Justice Clarence Thomas, 106th justice
Born: June 23, 1948; Pin Point, Georgia
Law school: Yale Law School
Appointed by: President George H. W. Bush
Sworn in: October 23, 1991

Associate Justice Ruth Bader Ginsburg, 107th justice
Born: March 15, 1933; Brooklyn, New York
Law school: Columbia Law School
Appointed by: President Bill Clinton
Sworn in: August 10, 1993

Associate Justice Stephen G. Breyer, 108th justice
Born: August 15, 1938; San Francisco, California
Law school: Harvard Law School
Appointed by: President Bill Clinton
Sworn in: August 3, 1994

Associate Justice Samuel Alito Jr., 110th justice
Born: April 1, 1950; Trenton, New Jersey
Law school: Yale Law School
Appointed by: President George W. Bush
Sworn in: January 31, 2006

Associate Justice Sonia Sotomayor, 111th justice
Born: June 25, 1954; Bronx, New York
Law school: Yale Law School
Appointed by: President Barack Obama
Sworn in: August 8, 2009

Associate Justice Elena Kagan, 112th justice
Born: April 28, 1960; New York, New York
Law school   : Harvard Law School
Appointed by: President Barack Obama
Sworn in: August 7, 2010

ALL MEMBERS OF THE SUPREME COURT
OF THE UNITED STATES

Name	State App't From	Appointed by	Judicial Oath Taken	Date Service Terminated
CHIEF JUSTICES				
Jay, John	NY	Washington	Oct. 19, 1789	Jun. 29, 1795
Rutledge, John	SC	Washington	Aug. 12, 1795	Dec. 15, 1795
Ellsworth, Oliver	CT	Washington	Mar. 8, 1796	Dec. 15, 1800
Marshall, John	VA	Adams, John	Feb. 4, 1801	Jul. 6, 1835
Taney, Roger Brooke	MD	Jackson	Mar. 28, 1836	Oct. 12, 1864
Chase, Salmon Portland	OH	Lincoln	Dec. 15, 1864	May 7, 1873
Waite, Morrison Remick	OH	Grant	Mar. 4, 1874	Mar. 23, 1888
Fuller, Melville Weston	IL	Cleveland	Oct. 8, 1888	Jul. 4, 1910
White, Edward Douglass	LA	Taft	Dec. 19, 1910	May 19, 1921
Taft, William Howard	CT	Harding	Jul. 11, 1921	Feb. 3, 1930
Hughes, Charles Evans	NY	Hoover	Feb. 24, 1930	Jun. 30, 1941
Stone, Harlan Fiske	NY	Roosevelt, F.	Jul. 3, 1941	Apr. 22, 1946
Vinson, Fred Moore	KY	Truman	Jun. 24, 1946	Sep. 8, 1953
Warren, Earl	CA	Eisenhower	Oct. 5, 1953	Jun. 23, 1969
Burger, Warren Earl	VA	Nixon	Jun. 23, 1969	Sep. 26, 1986
Rehnquist, William H.	VA	Reagan	Sep. 26, 1986	Sep. 3, 2005
Roberts, John G. Jr.	MD	Bush, G. W.	Sep. 29, 2005	
ASSOCIATE JUSTICES				
Rutledge, John	SC	Washington	Feb. 15, 1790	Mar. 5, 1791
Cushing, William	MA	Washington	Feb. 2, 1790	Sep. 13, 1810
Wilson, James	PA	Washington	Oct. 5, 1789	Aug. 21, 1798
Blair, John	VA	Washington	Feb. 2, 1790	Oct. 25, 1795
Iredell, James	NC	Washington	May 12, 1790	Oct. 20, 1799
Johnson, Thomas	MD	Washington	Aug. 6, 1792	Jan. 16, 1793
Paterson, William	NJ	Washington	Mar. 11, 1793	Sep. 9, 1806
Chase, Samuel	MD	Washington	Feb. 4, 1796	Jun. 19, 1811
Washington, Bushrod	VA	Adams, John	Feb. 4, 1799	Nov. 26, 1829
Moore, Alfred	NC	Adams, John	Apr. 21, 1800	Jan. 26, 1804
Johnson, William	SC	Jefferson	May 7, 1804	Aug. 4, 1834
Livingston, Henry Brockholst	NY	Jefferson	Jan. 20, 1807	Mar. 18, 1823
Todd, Thomas	KY	Jefferson	May 4, 1807	Feb. 7, 1826
Duvall, Gabriel	MD	Madison	Nov. 23, 1811	Jan. 14, 1835
Story, Joseph	MA	Madison	Feb. 3, 1812	Sep. 10, 1845

Name	State App't From	Appointed by	Judicial Oath Taken	Date Service Terminated
Thompson, Smith	NY	Monroe	Sep. 1, 1823	Dec. 18, 1843
Trimble, Robert	KY	Adams, J. Q.	Jun. 16, 1826	Aug. 25, 1828
McLean, John	OH	Jackson	Jan. 11, 1830	Apr. 4, 1861
Baldwin, Henry	PA	Jackson	Jan. 18, 1830	Apr. 21, 1844
Wayne, James Moore	GA	Jackson	Jan. 14, 1835	Jul. 5, 1867
Barbour, Philip Pendleton	VA	Jackson	May 12, 1836	Feb. 25, 1841
Catron, John	TN	Jackson	May 1, 1837	May 30, 1865
McKinley, John	AL	Van Buren	Jan. 9, 1838	Jul. 19, 1852
Daniel, Peter Vivian	VA	Van Buren	Jan. 10, 1842	May 31, 1860
Nelson, Samuel	NY	Tyler	Feb. 27, 1845	Nov. 28, 1872
Woodbury, Levi	NH	Polk	Sep. 23, 1845	Sep. 4, 1851
Grier, Robert Cooper	PA	Polk	Aug. 10, 1846	Jan. 31, 1870
Curtis, Benjamin Robbins	MA	Fillmore	Oct. 10, 1851	Sep. 30, 1857
Campbell, John Archibald	AL	Pierce	Apr. 11, 1853	Apr. 30, 1861
Clifford, Nathan	ME	Buchanan	Jan. 21, 1858	Jul. 25, 1881
Swayne, Noah Haynes	OH	Lincoln	Jan. 27, 1862	Jan. 24, 1881
Miller, Samuel Freeman	IA	Lincoln	Jul. 21, 1862	Oct. 13, 1890
Davis, David	IL	Lincoln	Dec. 10, 1862	Mar. 4, 1877
Field, Stephen Johnson	CA	Lincoln	May 20, 1863	Dec. 1, 1897
Strong, William	PA	Grant	Mar. 14, 1870	Dec. 14, 1880
Bradley, Joseph P.	NJ	Grant	Mar. 23, 1870	Jan. 22, 1892
Hunt, Ward	NY	Grant	Jan. 9, 1873	Jan. 27, 1882
Harlan, John Marshall	KY	Hayes	Dec. 10, 1877	Oct. 14, 1911
Woods, William Burnham	GA	Hayes	Jan. 5, 1881	May 14, 1887
Matthews, Stanley	OH	Garfield	May 17, 1881	Mar. 22, 1889
Gray, Horace	MA	Arthur	Jan. 9, 1882	Sep. 15, 1902
Blatchford, Samuel	NY	Arthur	Apr. 3, 1882	Jul. 7, 1893
Lamar, Lucius Quintus C.	MS	Cleveland	Jan. 18, 1888	Jan. 23, 1893
Brewer, David Josiah	KS	Harrison	Jan. 6, 1890	Mar. 28, 1910
Brown, Henry Billings	MI	Harrison	Jan. 5, 1891	May 28, 1906
Shiras, George Jr.	PA	Harrison	Oct. 10, 1892	Feb. 23, 1903
Jackson, Howell Edmunds	TN	Harrison	Mar. 4, 1893	Aug. 8, 1895
White, Edward Douglass	LA	Cleveland	Mar. 12, 1894	Dec. 18, 1910
Peckham, Rufus Wheeler	NY	Cleveland	Jan. 6, 1896	Oct. 24, 1909
McKenna, Joseph	CA	McKinley	Jan. 26, 1898	Jan. 5, 1925
Holmes, Oliver Wendell	MA	Roosevelt, T.	Dec. 8, 1902	Jan. 12, 1932
Day, William Rufus	OH	Roosevelt, T.	Mar. 2, 1903	Nov. 13, 1922

Name	State App't From	Appointed by	Judicial Oath Taken	Date Service Terminated
Moody, William Henry	MA	Roosevelt, T.	Dec. 17, 1906	Nov. 20, 1910
Lurton, Horace Harmon	TN	Taft	Jan. 3, 1910	Jul. 12, 1914
Hughes, Charles Evans	NY	Taft	Oct. 10, 1910	Jun. 10, 1916
Van Devanter, Willis	WY	Taft	Jan. 3, 1911	Jun. 2, 1937
Lamar, Joseph Rucker	GA	Taft	Jan. 3, 1911	Jan. 2, 1916
Pitney, Mahlon	NJ	Taft	Mar. 18, 1912	Dec. 31, 1922
McReynolds, James Clark	TN	Wilson	Oct. 12, 1914	Jan. 31, 1941
Brandeis, Louis Dembitz	MA	Wilson	Jun. 5, 1916	Feb. 13, 1939
Clarke, John Hessin	OH	Wilson	Oct. 9, 1916	Sep. 18, 1922
Sutherland, George	UT	Harding	Oct. 2, 1922	Jan. 17, 1938
Butler, Pierce	MN	Harding	Jan. 2, 1923	Nov. 16, 1939
Sanford, Edward Terry	TN	Harding	Feb. 19, 1923	Mar. 8, 1930
Stone, Harlan Fiske	NY	Coolidge	Mar. 2, 1925	Jul. 2, 1941
Roberts, Owen Josephus	PA	Hoover	Jun. 2, 1930	Jul. 31, 1945
Cardozo, Benjamin Nathan	NY	Hoover	Mar. 14, 1932	Jul. 9, 1938
Black, Hugo Lafayette	AL	Roosevelt, F.	Aug. 19, 1937	Sep. 17, 1971
Reed, Stanley Forman	KY	Roosevelt, F.	Jan. 31, 1938	Feb. 25, 1957
Frankfurter, Felix	MA	Roosevelt, F.	Jan. 30, 1939	Aug. 28, 1962
Douglas, William Orville	CT	Roosevelt, F.	Apr. 17, 1939	Nov. 12, 1975
Murphy, Frank	MI	Roosevelt, F.	Feb. 5, 1940	Jul. 19, 1949
Byrnes, James Francis	SC	Roosevelt, F.	Jul. 8, 1941	Oct. 3, 1942
Jackson, Robert Houghwout	NY	Roosevelt, F.	Jul. 11, 1941	Oct. 9, 1954
Rutledge, Wiley Blount	IA	Roosevelt, F.	Feb. 15, 1943	Sep. 10, 1949
Burton, Harold Hitz	OH	Truman	Oct. 1, 1945	Oct. 13, 1958
Clark, Tom Campbell	TX	Truman	Aug. 24, 1949	Jun. 12, 1967
Minton, Sherman	IN	Truman	Oct. 12, 1949	Oct. 15, 1956
Harlan, John Marshall	NY	Eisenhower	Mar. 28, 1955	Sep. 23, 1971
Brennan, William J. Jr.	NJ	Eisenhower	Oct. 16, 1956	Jul. 20, 1990
Whittaker, Charles Evans	MO	Eisenhower	Mar. 25, 1957	Mar. 31, 1962
Stewart, Potter	OH	Eisenhower	Oct. 14, 1958	Jul. 3, 1981
White, Byron Raymond	CO	Kennedy	Apr. 16, 1962	Jun. 28, 1993
Goldberg, Arthur Joseph	IL	Kennedy	Oct. 1, 1962	Jul. 25, 1965
Fortas, Abe	TN	Johnson, L.	Oct. 4, 1965	May 14, 1969
Marshall, Thurgood	NY	Johnson, L.	Oct. 2, 1967	Oct. 1, 1991
Blackmun, Harry A.	MN	Nixon	Jun. 9, 1970	Aug. 3, 1994
Powell, Lewis F. Jr.	VA	Nixon	Jan. 7, 1972	Jun. 26, 1987
Rehnquist, William H.	AZ	Nixon	Jan. 7, 1972	Sep. 26, 1986

Name	State App't From	Appointed by	Judicial Oath Taken	Date Service Terminated
Stevens, John Paul	IL	Ford	Dec. 19, 1975	Jun. 29, 2010
O'Connor, Sandra Day	AZ	Reagan	Sep. 25, 1981	Jan. 31, 2006
Scalia, Antonin	VA	Reagan	Sep. 26, 1986	
Kennedy, Anthony M.	CA	Reagan	Feb. 18, 1988	
Souter, David H.	NH	Bush, G. H. W.	Oct. 9, 1990	Jun. 29, 2009
Thomas, Clarence	GA	Bush, G. H. W.	Oct. 23, 1991	
Ginsburg, Ruth Bader	NY	Clinton	Aug. 10, 1993	
Breyer, Stephen G.	MA	Clinton	Aug. 3, 1994	
Alito, Samuel A. Jr.	NJ	Bush, G. W.	Jan. 31, 2006	
Sotomayor, Sonia	NY	Obama	Aug. 8, 2009	
Kagan, Elena	MA	Obama	Aug. 7, 2010	

Source: SupremeCourt.gov

MORE INFORMATION

C-SPAN'S *LANDMARK CASES*

Landmark Cases: Historic Supreme Court Decisions is a twelve-part television series debuting on C-SPAN in the fall of 2015. Produced in cooperation with the National Constitution Center, the series profiles a dozen significant cases from the country's founding through the 1973 decision in *Roe v. Wade* with a special emphasis on the human stories behind these rulings that have helped define the Court and shape our society.

The series airs live on C-SPAN and C-SPAN3, Mondays at 9 pm ET, beginning October 5, 2015. Once they have aired, all of the programs in the series will be archived, along with additional video, background information, and classroom resources, on the series website, **c-span.org/landmarkcases.**

C-SPAN

The cable television industry created C-SPAN in 1979, and C-SPAN2 in 1986, to provide gavel-to-gavel coverage of the U.S. House of Representatives and U.S. Senate. C-SPAN3 launched in 2001 to provide more choice in public affairs programming. Today our programming goes beyond Congress to include public affairs events from across the country as well as 48 hours of nonfiction books every weekend on C-SPAN2's Book TV, American History TV all weekend on C-SPAN3, and special history series like *Landmark Cases.*

c-span.org